Lewis Marshall Hagood

The Colored Man in the Methodist Episcopal Church

Lewis Marshall Hagood

The Colored Man in the Methodist Episcopal Church

ISBN/EAN: 9783337003401

Printed in Europe, USA, Canada, Australia, Japan

Cover: Foto ©Lupo / pixelio.de

More available books at **www.hansebooks.com**

Rev. L. M. HAGOOD, M. D.

THE COLORED MAN

IN THE

Methodist Episcopal Church.

BY

THE REV. L. M. HAGOOD, M. D.,
OF THE LEXINGTON CONFERENCE.

———◆———

CINCINNATI:
CRANSTON & STOWE.
NEW YORK:
HUNT & EATON.
1890.

PREFACE.

THE history of the relations existing ·between
the Methodist Episcopal Church and the colored man—or rather, the status of the colored man
within the Church—so far as known, has never been
written.   There are many cogent reasons why such
a history should be written.   From the time of the
landing of a cargo of twenty African slaves at
Jamestown, Virginia, in 1620, until this hour, the
colored man has been the subject of much discussion.   Touching his status as a man, there have
always been two sides: one in favor of enslaving
him, and the other objecting to enslaving him.
Both sides of this vexed question have always been
represented within the Church.   The fact that there
has always been a majority in the Church opposed
to enslaving him; that therefore the Church early en-
listed in the cause of his emancipation,—has kept
up a continuous though bloodless warfare within the
Church.

Thus the colored man early learned to love
Methodism, and soon large numbers were brought
into its communion. The emancipation and enfranchisement of the race did not put a quietus

upon the agitation of the question. Many white and colored members are not conversant with the history of our Church touching this subject. It has always been a question to many, why men of the race within the Church have not been as ready to write the *actual facts* in the case, as some of the race in other Churches have been to record many *half truths* relating thereto. It is true that while the public eye and ear appear always open and attentive to anything written or spoken by those who can claim kin with Jefferson, Clay, Sumner, Lincoln, or Grant, there is an apparent unwillingness to give audience to those who have always been subjected to ostracism.

These lines are written because it is believed that our Church has had to suffer because only *one side* of the story has been told by any person of the race, and in nearly, if not every instance, by those unfriendly to the relation the colored man has sustained to the Church; because some wrong impressions may be righted by the collation of facts that lay bare the glaring inaccuracies hitherto related concerning the imposition of the white members of the Church upon the colored; to show that, so far as the question goes, the heart of the Methodist Episcopal Church has always been right; and that, though errors may have been committed, they have been, in most instances, from the head and not from the heart of the Church; that it has come as near reaching the proper solution of the question,

"What shall be done with the colored man?" as any other organization that has had to do with the question.

There has been no intentional reflection or false or prejudicial statement made herein. Many "*stubborn facts*" have been left out, that might have been properly included. Though the story has not been told with the polished language of a Chesterfield, nor the logical acuteness of Aristotle, nor with the erudite diction of one born in the college, it is hoped that some good, and *no harm*, may be accomplished thereby; those of the race who have not had the opportunity to know some facts herein related may be enabled to teach their children that there is no need of blushing when the past history of the Church touching this question is being recited; but that it is a benefit to the race, as well as an honor, to be numbered with the million and a half members of the Methodist Episcopal Church.

CONTENTS.

CHAPTER X.

CHAPTER XI.

CHAPTER XII.

CHAPTER XIII.

CHAPTER XIV.

CHAPTER XV.

ILLUSTRATIONS.

INTRODUCTION.

IT is a difficult matter to write of a battle while it is still raging. The combatants are not usually the best judges of the merits of their cases. Prejudice, education, preconceived notions of the right or wrong in the case, prevent the mind from weighing the arguments with equity. There are principles lying at the foundation of ethics which will not be denied by Christians. They come with the authority of a "Thus saith the Lord." However distasteful these truths may be to the natural man, the obligation to receive them still remains. The Lord quoted certain proverbs which were authorities among the Jews, which they had observed as rules for their action towards others. One was "Thou shalt love thy neighbor, and hate thine enemy." Christ gives another, and with divine authority: "But I say unto you, Love your enemies, do good to them that hate you, and pray for them that despitefully use you and persecute you." Such teachings were not palatable in that day, any more than in the present. Human nature was no more ready to receive and practice such truths then than now. But the obligation existed then, and still survives. Then, too, the Savior taught another lesson equally unpalatable to the Jew. The man who fell among thieves was left by priest and Levite to suffer, but was delivered by the Samaritan, who was considered an enemy. "Who is my neighbor?" was the question that brought out this answer from Jesus with its illustration; viz., that every one needing help is a neighbor. The two great precepts of the same Teacher embrace all that is necessary in the practical treatment of the question of our relation to others: "Thou shalt love thy neighbor as thyself;" and, "Whatsoever ye would that men should do to you, do ye even so to them." Whatever apology there may have been for slavery in the past, in the days of ignorance, when God winked at it, as he did at polygamy, it is certain that the treatment of the slave as the New Testament requires would have destroyed slavery. To have educated the slave to read and write, and otherwise giving him the privilege to develop his mental faculties; to have secured him his wife—a God-given right; to have given these parents their rights, in obedience to the Divine command, to train up their children in the nurture and admonition of the Lord; to secure to them their right of a fair compensation for their labor, and to use it as they chose for their own benefit; to have granted them the privilege of worshiping their Maker as heaven required,—would have destroyed the whole system of involuntary servitude as it existed in these United States. More than two centuries slavery continued, while the enlightened conscience of the nation protested against the system, against the traffic in human beings, against its demoralizing influences on the white, and its degrading influence on the black man.

Methodism came into the country, and found slavery intrenched in its laws and civilization. Its preachers proclaimed a gospel of regeneration, of love to God, of a personal knowledge of forgiveness of sins, the witness of the Holy Ghost, of love to neighbors. The converts declared the religion of Christ: the "love that suffereth long and is kind." It turned out the old man and let in the new. White and black shared alike in the new life. Down in the cabin, up in the "great house," alike were heard the shouts of joy over this newfound pearl of great price. Tears of joy coursed down the ivory and the ebony cheek, as each spoke of redeeming love. Melted by this divine fire, fused into one spirit, there came to heart, to conscience, to understanding, as the white clasped the black hand with loving grip, the whispered voice of an inner consciousness, "Surely we be brethren." White Bishop Asbury declared the truth as it is in Christ Jesus, black Harry by his side preached the same gospel of the Son of God. The black messenger was honored by the divine presence attending his Word, as well as the white, and souls were saved when black Harry pointed sinners to the cross, as well as when the first bishop of the Methodist Episcopal Church called them to repentance.

Peter was astonished when he was sent to the Gentiles. He was more so when he saw them receive the gift of the Holy Ghost, and heard them declare the wonderful things of God. But he recognized them as brethren; and when his people at Jerusalem call him to account for his conduct in going among the Gentiles, he gives the history of the event, and sums it all up in these words: "Forasmuch then as God gave them the like gift as he did unto us, who believed on the Lord Jesus Christ, what was I that I could withstand God?" This settled the question for Peter, that the

Gentiles were entitled to all the rights and blessings of the Jew, as followers of Christ. If God honored the blacks with his Spirit's presence, filling them with joy and peace, enabling them to show forth the power of a Christian life in the fruits of holy living; if he anointed more than one black Harry "to preach good tidings unto the meek, to proclaim the acceptable year of the Lord," and honored their ministry in awakening and saving souls, is it a matter of wonder that there should be the conviction in the minds of Methodists that these slaves are men like ourselves? If men, then they are our neighbors; if our neighbors, then we must love them as ourselves. If we love them as men—as ourselves—then slavery, as it exists here, is wrong. The enlightened conscience of the Methodists said, " Slavery is wrong;" and this conviction was soon embodied in the question, which found its way into the Church law, and held its place there till it received its formal, practical answer in emancipation, " What shall be done for the extirpation of the evil of slavery ?"

The author of this book has treated of the relation of the Methodist Episcopal Church to the colored people from this stand-point of a clear perception of the evil of slavery, and the unrighteousness of one Christian holding his fellow-Christian, his brother in Christ, as a chattel. The writer traces the action of the law-making power of the Methodist Episcopal Church for nearly a hundred years, in her treatment of the colored man as a member of this Church, as an office-holder, and as a preacher under the system of slavery.

The author shows that the Methodist Episcopal Church has never swerved from the recognition of the rights of her colored members, in all her general and annual conferences. She denounced slavery as an evil to be extirpated, and at one time required her members to emancipate their slaves. (Had she adhered to her requirement, what a sea of wasted treasure, what a world of agony of the slave, what an ocean of bitter strife, and what a host of precious lives might have been saved!) She forbade the buying and selling slaves; she tried to enforce rules for the merciful treatment of the bondmen; she made provision to have all of the gospel preached to them that the masters would allow or the preacher thought safe. She did what she could to have the relation of husband and wife duly recognized. He also tells us that, as soon as the sounds of battle had ceased, this Church began her work again among the colored people. She organized them into Churches, took their own men and made them pastors; although poorly qualified for this work, received them into conferences with their white brethren, and gave them all the rights and privileges of members and ministers of the Methodist Episcopal Church.

The reluctance of some to accept the situation of Negro equality in the Church led to the discussion of the question, What shall we do with the Negro? The author gives the outline of this discussion and the action of the Church authorities in reference to it. The unwillingness to recognize the manhood and brotherhood of the Negro on the part of some members and ministers of the Church, gave rise to such treatment of the colored brethren that they were easily persuaded that the white brethren did not want to be associated with them in Church or conference relation. Hence, when

the white brethren asked the colored to go out of
the conferences and set up for themselves, the colored brethren did so, not always because they thought
it absolutely best, but best under the circumstances;
not because they thought it right, but because they
were disposed to yield to the desires of the white brethren. The reasons for the treatment of the Negro are
very much the same as the grounds for neglect of
the poor, ignorant, and degraded of any community.
People do not like to come in contact with the unculti-
vated in intellect and morals. Hence the fine church,
where it is written in the dress and bearing of the wor-
shipers, ''No poor are desired here.'' Hence the mission Churches, where the action of both the poor and
the wealthy members of the Church says: ''No rich are
expected here.'' There is a disposition to separate the
Christian Church into classes corresponding to classes in
social life. The distinctions, so marked in society, are
carried into the Church. In the case of the Negro, this
feeling against the ignorance, uncouthness, which is
found in the lowest strata of whites, is intensified by
two circumstances, which belong exclusively to the
Negro. The first is the color. There exists more or
less color repugnance in most persons not accustomed
to seeing colored people. There is less objection to
having colored persons about them among the Southern people than the Northern. The Southern women
largely let the slaves nurse their children, and many of
the prominent Southern men and women speak very
kindly of their Negro mammies—color repugnance is not
instinctive. The second great cause of the unwillingness to treat the Negro as an equal, in State and

Church is, no doubt, his former condition of servitude. That it is not altogether his color is evident from the treatment that the Indian, the Hindoo, or the Japanese receives, many of whom are as dark as the great mass of the Negroes. He was a slave, kept a slave, and wronged by the white man. One of the hardest things for poor human nature to do is to confess a wrong and make restitution. That slavery is wrong, is recognized by all the action of the Methodist Episcopal Church on that subject; and the question should be, How can we best atone for the wrong, and remove from the Negro, as speedily as possible, all the effects of this wrong?

That the Negro is an inferior part of the human family is stoutly asserted by some people, though it has never been proved. Suppose, for the moment, we admit it; granted that the Negro is inferior in some respects, no matter what; then we ask, Does this misfortune entitle the more gifted part of God's family to the right of treating the unfortunate ones unjustly, of depriving them of liberty, of the pursuit of happiness? Does the misfortune of the hunchback entitle the straight ones to the privilege of abusing him? Does the cripple, on his crutches, entitle the strong to the right of elbowing him out of the way? Do not these very misfortunes demand our sympathy and kindly offices? Why not? If the Negro is unfortunate, let him have our kindness instead of our kicks? The caricatures of the Negro, seen in the public prints, have their influence in confirming this low estimate of the colored people.

The history of the Methodist Episcopal Church, in her ecclesiastical action, is generally worthy of commendation. There are, however, cases of individual action that are not creditable to these persons or societies, either as patriots, philanthropists, or Christians. The Protestant Churches should be as open to the Negro as to any other division of the human family. The public places should be as easy of access to them as to others. They should receive just as much for their money as the white, red, or brown man. This is not in the power of the Methodist Episcopal Church to bestow; but the membership should bear in mind that with God there is no respect of persons. The utterances which the Methodist Episcopal Church has made are all demanded by the enlightenment of the nineteenth century. What is needed is for the practice to correspond with these utterances. Why should the Negro be ostracized any more than any other member of the human family? Why should our Churches and schools be closed to him? Why should he be compelled to ride in the smoking-car, when he pays for first-class accommodations? Why driven from our hotels, and forced to seek shelter in private families? Why are the colored ministers and members of the Methodist Episcopal Church compelled to endure these wrongs? The author might have called attention to the fact that this Church, with its millions of members and adherents, with its press and its pulpits, has never raised her mighty voice in a grand protest against these wrongs perpetrated against a quarter of a million of her membership. What is needed, perhaps, most of all, is to regard the Negro as belonging to the human family, and treat him as such. The social question, which is protruded upon all occasions, must not be a matter of legislation; each individual must settle that for himself. An intelligent Negro lady, when asked by a white man, "Shall we admit the Negro to our parlors?" replied, "If you white gentlemen will stay out of our parlors, we will stay out of yours." The social bugbear, that is constantly bandied about in this discussion, has no more to do with the recognition of the rights of the Negro than has the question of the annexation of Canada. The author has given facts of history which all the Church should know; and, knowing, they will have no reason to be ashamed of the record of the Methodist Episcopal Church. This subject demands the honest, earnest consideration of the membership of the entire Christian Church, and specially of the membership of the Methodist Episcopal Church. The fact that there are nearly a quarter of a million of her members who have as much right to recognition in her sanctuaries as any other class of men, who are invited and urged to go off by themselves, and be ignorant teachers of ignorant scholars, because the Heavenly Father has given them a little darker dress, and because they have been more abused and wronged than any other part of the human family, is not creditable to those who profess to be governed by the Golden Rule. The Church should see to it that the colored members of her communion may feel at home in her churches, whether they be stone-front palaces in the metropolis of the nation or cabins in the swamps or mountains of the South. To bring this about, the Methodist Episcopal Church has not done all she can. Theoretically, the utterances are all right, but the practice must be brought up to the theory. The press and the pulpit should give no uncertain sound. The conferences, annual as well as General, should be exemplifications of the brotherhood of man and the Fatherhood of God. This book will wake up thought on a subject ou which the membership of the Methodist Episcopal Church need to think and to act. The millions of colored people in this country need to be held close to the heart of Protestant Christianity, so they will be found on the side of the Church of God in the struggle for the conquest of this world for Christ. The book well merits a careful reading, as the author speaks from the stand-point of an intelligent appreciation of the treatment of the Negro, as he has had some personal experiences which entitle him to be heard. He writes clearly, and presents his case forcibly, yet without bitterness, and recognizes gratefully what the Methodist Episcopal Church has done for the colored man. The spirit of the writer is commendable, although the conflict is not ended, and he is one of the combatants.

JOHN BRADEN.

CENTRAL TENNESSEE COLLEGE,
    NASHVILLE, TENN., 1889.

THE COLORED MAN

IN THE

METHODIST EPISCOPAL CHURCH.

———•———

CHAPTER I.

BEFORE THE WAR.

FROM time immemorial men have differed upon nearly every phase of human existence; and, for that matter, every other kind of existence. So far as we know, no organization has ever existed, formed by man, or formed by Deity for man (it makes no difference for what purpose it was formed), in which there was not manifested individuality to the point of wide divergence on most important questions. Unconverted human nature is the same the world over, and different propensities and dispositions, coupled with jealousy, have manifested themselves in nearly every family since that of the first pair driven in shame from Eden.

As strange as it may sound, the Church of God has been no exception to this rule in general, nor the Methodist Episcopal Church in particular. The Methodist Episcopal Church was born of necessity, and has perpetuated itself and prospered in proportion as it has obeyed the mandates of Almighty God. When, for any reason, the Church has turned to the right hand or to the left hand out of "the king's highway," God has gently reproved her. It was but a short time after its organization when it became a recognized, potent factor in God's hands of ameliorating the condition of those with whom it had influence. No other Church, since its organization in this country, has figured more conspicuously than the Methodist Episcopal Church in all the living, burning questions touching the salvation of men's bodies and souls. It may be true that in many instances the Church has not come up to the ideal of some of its devotees, or accomplished all it was considered able to do. Probably instances would have occurred, if it had succeeded in the former, when it would have displeased God; if the latter, it might have bound error with a rope of sand, and thus frustrated all effective plans.

From the beginning the Church has gone after "the lost sheep of the house of Israel." A Church needs no higher encomium than that the "common people" hear her ministers gladly. This has been, and we hope now is, the glory of the Methodist Episcopal Church. Should a time ever come when this can not be truthfully said of the Church, her pristine glory will have departed. Worldly popularity has not hitherto been the acme of her ambition. May it never be! Where duty called, popular or unpopular, the Church has given the command, "Go forward," with the understanding that "it is better to obey God than man." The wholesome doctrine of "the Fatherhood of God and the brotherhood of man," as taught by the apostle when he exclaimed, "God hath made of one blood all nations of men for to dwell on all the face of the earth," has been taught by the Methodist Episcopal Church ever since John Wesley declared slavery "the sum of all villainies."

It may be, as you scrutinize the last sentence, a fear may arise that it will not remain intact under the electric light of investigation. The redeeming feature is, that the Methodist Episcopal Church has come as near preaching and practicing that doctrine as any other American ecclesiastical organization. This may not be much in its favor, when taken in reference to the colored man, but it *is* something. There has never been an hour since Bishop Asbury preached Jesus and him crucified to a poor slave on the bank of a river in South Carolina, in the which the great heart of the Methodist Episcopal Church did not throb with sympathy for the poor colored man in this country. As evidence, it is only necessary to look up or remember the Herculean efforts it made on his behalf as early as 1796, to save him from the cruelty and barbarism of his subjection. Could the Church, at so early a period, have received the moral and religious support of the good people of other denominations, the civil war might have been averted, and the poor slave rescued from the power of Satan unto God, from the midnight of sin to the marvelous light and liberty of the gospel of Jesus Christ.

The following explains itself on this question, as enacted by the *General Conference of 1796:*

" *Question.* What regulations shall be made for the extirpation of the crying evil of African slavery?

" *Answer* 1. We declare, that we are more than ever convinced of the great evil of the African slavery which still exists in these United States; and do most earnestly recommend to the yearly conferences, quarterly meetings, and to those who have the oversight of districts and circuits, to be exceedingly cautious what persons they admit to official stations in our Church; and, in the case of future admission to official stations, to require such security of those who hold slaves, for the emancipation of them, immediately or gradually, as the laws of the States respectively, and the circumstances of the case will admit. And we do fully authorize all the yearly conferences to make whatever regulations they judge proper, in the present case, respecting the admission of persons to official stations in our Church.

" 2. No slaveholder shall be received into society till the preacher who has the oversight of the circuit has spoken to him freely and faithfully on the subject of slavery.

" 3. Every member of the society who sells a slave shall immediately, after full proof, be excluded the society. And if any member of our society purchase a slave, the ensuing quarterly meeting shall determine on the number of years in which the slave so purchased would work out the price of his purchase. And the person so purchasing shall, immediately after such determination, execute a legal instrument for the manumission of such slave at the expiration of the term determined by the quarterly meeting. And in default of his executing such instrument of manumission, or on his refusal to submit his case to the judgment of the quarterly meeting, such member shall be excluded the society. Provided, also, that in the case of a female slave, it shall be inserted in the aforesaid instrument of manumission, that all her children which shall be born during the years of her servitude shall be free at the following times, namely: Every female child at the age of twenty-one, and every male child at the age of twenty-five. Nevertheless, if the member of our society, executing the said instrument of manumission, judge it proper, he may fix the times of manumission of the children of the female slaves beforementioned, at an earlier age than that which is prescribed above.

"4. The preachers and other members of our society are requested to consider the subject of Negro slavery with deep attention till the ensuing General Conference; and that they impart to the General Conference, through the medium of the yearly conferences, or otherwise, any important thoughts upon the subject, that the conference may have full light, in order to take further steps toward eradicating this enormous evil from that part of the Church of God to which they are united."

During the ensuing quadrennium this all-important question was argued and studied as never before within the Church. Considerable feeling was manifested in many instances, showing at once the deep interest the question had produced. Men within and without the Church continued to examine the question, until the question of the continuation of human slavery became *the* question of the hour. More than one slaveholding member of the Church declared, with all the earnestness of his soul, that it was unwise for the Church to shoulder such a stupendous burden. Others declared it would be suicidal for the General Conference to interfere with the deep-rooted institution of slavery. As the quadrennium advanced, the question was more vehemently agitated. Many tried to conjecture what action the ensuing General Conference of 1800 would take on this subject, while others tried to forestall any anticipated action. It was openly declared by the more sanguine slaveholders within the Church that the General Conference would pay no attention to the question of slavery; that in the event that memorials or resolutions should be presented touching the question, they would at once be referred to a committee, which would fail to notice them. Others as hopefully and boldly declared that no Christian Church could be consistent and indorse human slavery; that the future hope of the Church in its effort to spread Scriptural holiness was dependent, in a measure, upon the attitude it sustained toward human slavery.

Those who have engaged in the heated discussions that have arisen within the General Conferences since that day, upon questions growing out of the system of slavery in this country, can probably imagine the situation at that time. The General Conference of 1800 sat from the 6th to the 20th of May, in Baltimore. Delegates from each of the eight annual conferences were present. Each delegate saw the ominous clouds, and knew the storm was brewing. This question soon came up for consideration. We give as near as possible a detailed account of the proceedings touching the question of slavery:

GENERAL CONFERENCE, 1800.—"Brother Ormond moved, That whereas the laws now in force in two or more of the United States pointedly prohibit the emancipation of slaves, and the third clause of the ninth section of the Discipline forbids the selling of slaves, it is evident that the members of the Methodist societies who own slaves, and remove themselves and families to another State, or to distant parts of the same State, and leave a husband or a wife behind, held in bondage by another person, part man and wife, which is a violation of the righteous laws of God, and contrary to the peace and happiness of families; and whereas, it is further observed that the rule now existing among us prevents our members increasing the number of their slaves by purchase, and tolerates an increase of number by birth, which children are often given to the enemy of the Methodists,—my mind being seriously impressed with these and several other considerations, I move, That this General Conference take the momentous subject of slavery into consideration, and make such alterations in the old rule as may be thought proper.

"Brother Timmons moved, That if any of our traveling preachers marry persons holding slaves, and thereby become slaveholders, they shall be excluded from our societies, unless they execute a legal emancipation of their slaves, agreeably to the laws of the State wherein they live. Superseded.

Friday Morning, May 16th.—" Brother Snethen moved, That this General Conference do resolve, that from this time forth no slaveholder shall be admitted into the Methodist Episcopal Church. Negatived.

"Brother Bloodgood moved, That all Negro children belonging to the members of the Methodist society, who shall be born in slavery after the fourth day of July, 1800, shall be emancipated—males at — years, and females at — years. Negatived.

"Brother Lathomus moved, That every member of the Methodist Episcopal Church holding slaves shall, within the term of one year from the date hereof, give an instrument of emancipation for all his slaves, and the quarterly-meeting conference shall determine on the time the slaves shall serve, if the laws of the State do not expressly prohibit their emancipation. Negatived.

"Moved, That when any of our traveling preachers become owners of a slave or slaves by any means, they shall forfeit their ministerial character in the Methodist Episcopal Church, unless they execute, if it be practicable, a legal emancipation of such slave or slaves, agreeably to the laws of the State wherein they live. Agreed to."

This motion was originally offered by Brother Timmons, and was conceived by the secretary to have been superseded in the progress of the business upon slavery. But the conference voted that they would act upon it, with the amendments, the same as a new motion.

It can be plainly seen by the foregoing report into what a strait the General Conference was brought by this question, as well as how earnestly and faithfully that General Conference strove to ascertain "the mind of the Holy Spirit" as to the question. Just think of the fact that in *one day* of that General Conference six different phases of this question were presented. Amid these were: (1) To prevent the separation of husband and wife; (2) To change a former rule that allowed a Methodist to buy a husband or wife when they belonged to separate parties, so as to prevent a separation. Even in this form the buying and selling of human beings was objected to strenuously. It was considered "doing evil, that good might come therefrom."

As we stop to contemplate it, we shudder to render a decision. They voted down every proposition that looked in any way like buying or selling human beings. It is not superstition to say, they attempted to "avoid even the appearance of evil." They consented to allow, (1) The expulsion of *any minister* of the Church "who shall marry a woman owning slaves;" (2) No slaveholder to be received into the Church; (3) All traveling preachers who owned slaves to forfeit their ministerial character. It is no wonder that such action was taken, when it is remembered that the Church was even then recognizing and licensing colored local ministers, and employing them to preach. It now concluded not only nominally to recognize local preachers, but to ordain them as well. As early as 1784, at "the Christmas conference," rules prohibiting slavery had been enacted. And these rules were not simply hanging about the necks of slaveholders as mere ornaments; for it was positively declared by the Church, "every person concerned, who will not comply with these rules, shall have the privilege quietly to withdraw." We know of *no instance* in the history of the Church in which there has ever been a single human being directly driven from her ranks, pews, or pulpit because of race, color, or previous condition of servitude. Then why wonder when such a Church ordains one of her sons, and sends him forth to tell with simplicity the story of the cross?

Many objected to going so far with the slaves, for fear of offending the slaveholder. But the Church paid no attention to such cries; hence the following action was taken by the General Conference, under the heading

"A REGULATION *respecting the ordination of colored people to the office of deacons:*

"The bishops have obtained leave, by the suffrages of this General Conference, to ordain local deacons of our African brethren in places where they have built a house or houses for the worship of God: *Provided,* they have a person among them qualified for that office, and he can obtain an election of two-thirds of the male members of the society to which he belongs, and a recommendation from the minister who has the charge, and his fellow-laborers in the city or circuit."

This action at once recognized the efforts of the race at elevation, and gave the colored people to understand, that though in bondage to earthly taskmasters, they were fellow-heirs of the inheritance of the saints, heirs of God, and joint heirs with Jesus Christ, the righteous. The gainsaying, slaveholding world stood aghast as it read and re-read the action taken by that General Conference on the question of human slavery. God pulled back, as it were, the curtains of the upper world, and blandly smiled approval. A general baptism of the Holy Ghost ratified the action in that such a revival of religion followed that again the world cried, as Methodist preachers began to preach Jesus and him crucified: "They that have turned the world upside down are come hither also."

In the General Conference that met in the city of Baltimore, Md., from May 7th to 28th, 1804, much discussion was had on the question of slavery. Notwithstanding other questions of Church polity claimed the attention of this conference to such a degree that Bishop Asbury refused to vote on one of the questions put, the conference sympathized with the colored man enough to legislate in his behalf.

A variety of motions were proposed on the subject of slavery, and, after a long conversation, Freeborn Garrettson moved "that the subject of slavery be left to the three bishops to form a section to suit the Southern and Northern States, as they in their wisdom may think best, to be submitted to this conference." This motion was submitted to the conference, and was carried.

The report of the Committee on Slavery which, with amendments, was adopted by the Conference, and forms section nine, "Of Slavery," reads:

"1. We declare, that we are as much as ever convinced of the great evil of slavery, and do most earnestly recommend to the yearly conferences, quarterly-meeting conferences, and to those who have the oversight of districts, circuits, and stations, to be exceedingly cautious what persons they admit to official stations in our Church, and in the case of future admission to official stations, to require such security of those who hold slaves, for the emancipation of them, immediately or gradually, as the laws of the States respectively and the circumstances of the case will admit; and we do fully authorize all the yearly conferences to make whatever regulations they judge proper in the present case respecting the admission of persons to official stations in our Church.

"2. When any traveling preacher becomes the owner of a slave, or slaves, by any means, he shall forfeit his ministerial character in our Church, unless he execute, if it be practicable, a legal emancipation of such slaves, conformably to the laws of the State in which he lives.

"3. No slaveholder shall be received in full membership in our society till the preacher who has the oversight of the circuit or station has spoken to him fully and faithfully on the subject of slavery.

"4. Every member of our society who sells a slave, except at the request of the slave, in cases of mercy or humanity, agreeably to the judgment of a committee of three male members of the society, appointed by the preacher who has the charge of the circuit or station, shall, immediately after full proof, be excluded the society; and if any members of our society purchase a slave, the ensuing quarterly-meeting conference shall determine on the number of years which the slave so purchased should serve to work out the price of his purchase; and the person so purchasing shall, immediately after such determination, execute a legal instrument for the manumission of such slave at the expiration of the time determined by the quarterly-meeting conference; and in default of his executing such instrument of manumission, or on his refusal to submit his case to the judgment of the quarterly-meeting conference, such member shall be excluded the society: *Provided,* that in the case of a female slave, it shall be inserted in the aforesaid instrument of manumission that all her children who shall be born during the years of her servitude shall be free at the following times, viz.; every female child at the age of twenty-one, and every male child at the age of twenty-five: *Provided,* also, that if a member of our society shall buy a slave with a certificate of future emancipation, the terms of emancipation shall, notwithstanding, be subject to the decision of the quarterly-meeting conference. Nevertheless, the members of our societies in the States of North Carolina, South Carolina, and Georgia shall be exempted from the operations of the above rules.

"5. Let our preachers from time to time, as occasion serves, admonish and exhort all slaves to render due respect and obedience to the commands and interests of their respective masters."

The intention of the whole of the foregoing resolutions in general, and the last part in particular, was to preserve peace between master and slave, and prohibit the former from having occasion to chastise the latter, because the latter might use his religious privileges to his own harm. Though the Church had already a fixed purpose and established regulations touching the question of slavery, the General Conference of 1808, held in Baltimore, Md., from May 6th to 26th, discussed it, and took action upon it again. An effort was adroitly made to change certain paragraphs in the Discipline against slavery. The following settled the question at that General Conference. It was moved, by Stephen G. Roszel, and seconded by Thomas Ware, "That the first two paragraphs of the section on slavery be retained in our Discipline, and that the General Conference authorize each annual conference to form their own regulations relative to buying and selling slaves." The motion was carried.

During the ensuing quadrennium the question of slavery was not agitated to any great degree. While the one faction rested upon its laurels, the defeated faction was recuperating its numerical strength pursuant to another attack.

At the General Conference of 1812, nothing of importance on this question was done or needed to be done, more than had already been accomplished.

The city of New York, where the General Conference was held, had in it the oldest Methodist Episcopal Church, the John St. Church. Among its
first members were colored people, who had worshiped there in peace all along. Philadelphia,
where a number of colored people resided, had long
been celebrated as "the City of Churches." Colored and white Methodists for years had worshiped together there in peace. But now a storm
was brewing that threatened not only to inundate the
Church, but the roaring thunder of which would
likely rend the Church in twain, so far as the two
races within it were concerned.

CHAPTER II.

THE COLOR-LINE SECESSIONS.

WHEN it is remembered that the African slave-trade in this country was intrenched behind the venerated Constitution, it is not strange that nearly every conflict the Methodist Episcopal Church has had touching slavery aroused bitter opposition within and without the Church. In most instances it is conceded that defeated or desperate enemies, when opposing a third inveterate foe, will, if an opportunity is afforded, unite against a common enemy; or, in other words, Pilate and Herod will unite. Working out from within is often found the more effectual way, whether it be a prison, a political or ecclesiastical party, or the disruption of a Church. It was thus done in the secession of colored members from our Church in 1816 and 1820. Among the number of colored members belonging to St. George's Methodist Episcopal Church of Philadelphia in 1815 was a local preacher, Richard Allen, who afterward organized and became the first bishop of the "Bethel Connection," afterwards known as "the African Methodist Episcopal Church." The colored members, under his leadership, formed a nucleus of a society for themselves, aside from, and out of the jurisdiction of, the pastor of St. George's Church. The entire affair was local, and the result of the dissatisfaction that arose was the same as it would be to-day if a local preacher, white or colored, were to organize a society in opposition to the wishes of his pastor, purchase Church property for the congregation, or part of it, and then deed it to a few individuals instead of the Church. It has been intimated by persons whose reputation rests more or less upon that and similar transactions, that it was the outgrowth of neglect on the part of pastor and people of St. George's Church. Let Bishop Allen answer that question. He says: "I was then working for George Giger. Before this, Bishop Asbury asked me to travel with him. The bishop proffered me what he was receiving, my victuals and clothes." Rev. R. Allen refused this offer, as he says: "I told him that I thought people ought to lay up something while they were able, to support themselves in time of sickness and old age. But I made up my mind that I would not accept of his proposals. Shortly after, I left Hartford Circuit and came to Pennsylvania, on Lancaster Circuit. I traveled several months on this circuit with the Revs. Peter Moriarty and Ira Ellis. The elder in charge in Philadelphia frequently sent for me to come to the city. February, 1786, I came to Philadelphia. Preaching was given out for me for five o'clock A. M., in St. George's Church. I strove to preach as well as I could, but it was a great cross to me; but the Lord was with me. We had a good time, and several souls were awakened, and were earnestly seeking redemption in the blood of Christ. I thought I would stop in Philadelphia a week or two. I preached at different places in the city. My labor was much blessed; I soon saw a large field open in seeking and instructing my African brethren. I preached wherever I could find an opening. I established prayer-meetings; I raised a society in 1786 of forty-two members. I saw the necessity of erecting a place of worship for the colored people of the city; but here I met opposition. But three colored brethren united with me in erecting a place of worship."

Now let us rest and contemplate for a moment the situation. Here we find a local preacher of the Methodist Episcopal Church was invited by the pastor and presiding elder of St. George's Methodist Episcopal Church to come to the city, and preach to his congregation at an usual hour for service, five A. M. He came; success attended his labors. He then, encouraged by success, began going hither and thither to preach in the city. He, of course, found a following. What effort of the kind was ever made that did not find a following? Does it appear a repetition of the story of Absalom? But let us not stop now to consider that phase of it. In St. George's Church, though welcomed, he "found it a cross to preach" there. Why was it a cross to preach the gospel there? Have we not in the above sentence a key to the entire situation? Was it not the effort to avoid having to preach to those who had formed an idea of what a sermon should be from the ministrations of the pulpit of St. George's Church that brought about the other complaints? Do not such things grow? Rev. Richard Allen had preached but a short time to his "African brethren" until a *necessity* for a separate Church arose. He says himself that the leading colored members refused to go with him. It was natural, therefore, that the above-mentioned *necessity* would arise. Why was it that, as he determined to form another society and erect a church, when he presented the project " to the most respectable colored people of Philadelphia, they bitterly opposed it?" Now, if it was entirely regular, Christ-like, and therefore right, why was it that but three colored men—Absalom Jones, William White, and Darius Ginnings—would unite in that project? Rev. Richard Allen says: "These united with me as soon as it became public and known by the elder, who was stationed in the city." Why this secrecy? Who were instigating, abetting, and encouraging Richard Allen in this move? Let us suppose it was members of another denomination in that city, or some of the white members of St. George's Church. They could only have taken sides and pushed the matter, because, (1) They opposed meeting and worshiping with colored people, and could use him—Mr. Allen—to help them; or, (2) They opposed the pastor of St. George's Church, and wanted a complaint against him; or, (3) They believed the colored members of St. George's Church were being imposed upon by the white members; or, (4) They wished to germinate schism within St. George's Church. If the colored members were being imposed upon, could Mr. Allen not have remedied the matter by remaining and combining the strength of the imposed upon with that of the good white members of St. George, and fighting the matter to the end?

But Rev. Richard Allen capitulated. Is capitulation on the part of a general attacked an exhibition of leadership or prowess? General Sigel, in the late war, became famous at it; but only among a certain class of soldiers. When it is remembered that our African brethren were in such a fort as St. George's, the capitulation seems to take on the air of cowardice. Instead of that Church being a monument and outgrowth of a desire of our white members to *drive* the black ones out, it is just the opposite—the outgrowth of an effort to *keep them within our communion.* Mr. Allen, after reciting his action in the premises, relates what followed. One conversant with the polity of our Church, after knowing what had gone before, can shut his eyes and tell what followed, especially if the presiding elder, Dr. Roberts, and our pastor, then stationed at St. George's Church, knew and dared do their duty. Nothwithstanding this, as strange as it may appear, we hear from the lips of some ministers of the African Methodist Episcopal Church that their dear African brethren, members of St. George's Church, "were pulled off their knees while at prayer in the church, because of their color;" nearly every young minister entering some of their conferences, ignorant of Methodist history, gives the above answer to the question, why he prefers *that* connection to all others. Of course, the tyro knows nothing to the contrary. It is known by every one conversant with our history, that even after the "Allenites," as they were called, had gone out and erected a building for Church purposes, the presiding elder and pastor of St. George's Church were willing to let them go on with their separate worship, not exercising, or desiring to exercise, a tithe as much authority over them as almost any one of their own presiding elders does over their Churches in this country to-day. The presiding elder, having an appointment to preach for them one Sabbath, was surprised to hear them exclaim as he walked up the aisle of their church that day, " Pray, brethren, pray ; here comes the devil !" Such language as that in God's house shows the *animus* that actuated that side of this question. With such a spirit actuating them, the matter could hardly have been settled otherwise than it was, or they had to remain under the supervision of our Church. The question has often been asked if Richard Allen was in the Church on the occasion when that outcry was made. The answer has been, time and again, that "*he first began the cry.*"

When it is remembered that the "Absalom Jones" mentioned as having joined Richard Allen in this movement, was *a priest in the Protestant Episcopal Church*, and that Richard Allen had acquired considerable wealth, more light falls on the dark background. Notwithstanding the fact that many thousands of colored members had joined the Methodist Episcopal Church, and were considered in general orderly and exemplary members, some of the more intelligent males possessing gifts, grace, and usefulness, as such, had been licensed, and several ordained deacons and elders, and that the colored members under Richard Allen had formed an organization, having built a respectable church and were under the oversight of one of our white presiding elders, they were restless, and chafed in the harness. In April, 1816, one month before the session of the General Conference that met in Baltimore, upwards of *one thousand colored members*, under the leadership of Richard Allen, had withdrawn from our Church. Why? A General Conference was called immediately after the formation of a Church by Rev. Richard Allen, and *he* was elected their first bishop! The most wonderful thing concerning this whole affair is the *constant, regular succession of events!* These, however, are the straws in the winds. It is, therefore, but little distance to the prime cause of that secession. Of the 42,304 colored members remaining in the Church during the quadrennium, many of them were, praying that the unpleasant episode at Philadelphia would end there, and give the Church peace. Notwithstanding the trouble with the Allenites, as they were called, the Church still sympathized with the race, and the Committee on Slavery at the General Conference gave no sound for retreat from the vantage ground assumed. The whole report read thus:

"The committee to whom was referred the business of slavery beg leave to report that they have taken the subject into serious consideration, and, after mature deliberation, they are of opinion that, under the present existing circumstances in relation to slavery, little can be done to abolish a practice so contrary to the principles of moral justice. They are sorry to say that the evil appears to be past remedy, and they are led to deplore the destructive consequences which have already accrued, and are yet likely to result therefrom.

"Your committee find that in the South and West the civil authorities render emancipation impracticable, and notwithstanding they are led to fear that some of our members are too easily contented with laws so unfriendly to freedom, yet, nevertheless, they are constrained to admit that to bring about such a change in the civil code as would favor the cause of liberty is not in the power of the General Conference. Your committee have attentively read and seriously considered a memorial on the above subject, presented from several persons within the bounds of the Baltimore Annual Conference. They have also made inquiry into the regulations adopted and pursued by the different annual conferences in relation to this subject, and they find that some of them have made no efficient rules on the subject of slavery, thereby leaving our people to act as they please, while others have adopted rules and pursued courses not a little different from each other, all pleading the authority given them by the General Conference, according to our present existing rule, as stated in our form of Discipline. Your committee conclude that, in order to be consistent and uniform, the rule should be express and definite, and, to bring about this uniformity, they beg leave to submit the following resolution :

" *Resolved*, by the delegates of the annual conferences in General Conference assembled, That all the recommendatory part of the second division, ninth section, and first answer of our form of Discipline after the word 'slavery,' be stricken out, and the following words inserted: 'Therefore, no slaveholder shall be eligible to any official station in our Church hereafter, where the laws of the State in which he lives will admit of emancipation, and and permit the liberated slave to enjoy freedom.'"

soon a feeling began to show itself, from some
cause, that it was "degrading for them in any way
to be dependent upon white folks for the administration of the ordinances and the government
of the Church." During this year, as before, every
effort was made by the Church to remove all these
complaints. Concession after concession was made,
but all to no purpose. The removal of the supposed evil was not the desideratum with the pro-
voking cause. Notwithstanding they were har-
assed until they left the Church, instead of uniting
with Richard Allen's faction, they chose to establish a Church of their own. Some say they did not
have full confidence in Rev. R. Allen. In 1819
they decided to withdraw from the Methodist
Episcopal Church. The fact that our Church had
not recognized colored men as traveling preachers
was the complaint under which they left. By this
secession we lost fourteen local preachers, and nearly
one thousand members, including class-leaders,
exhorters, and stewards. Notwithstanding many
strange stories originated with or grew out of these
secessions, the Rev. N. Bangs, the second Methodist
historian, expresses the feelings of our Church
when he said: "We can not do otherwise than
wish them all spiritual and temporal blessings in
Christ Jesus. Though formally separated from us
in name, we still love them as our spiritual children, and stand ready to aid them, as far as we may,
in extending the Redeemer's kingdom among men."

If these secessions had occurred among those who were in bondage, it might have appeared less strange. If those who led them had even professed the belief that the secession would ameliorate the condition of the suffering millions of the race then in bondage in the South, it might have assumed the role of race pride. But, alas! the condition of the poor slave in the South, whose interests every General Conference, and the one soon to meet in the city of Baltimore, had carefully considered and did all it could to emancipate him, was not written in their bond. *Those secessions did nothing toward bettering the condition of the slaves at the South.* If they did anything touching human slavery then existing in this country, it was to leave the suspicion of ungratefulness on the face of every struggling slave in the South. It is but a truism to say, it strengthened the belief that the race did not thank the Methodist Episcopal Church for what it was even then trying to do for them, and yet, notwithstanding this, the following was the action of the *General Conference of 1824:*

" *Resolved,* 1. That all our preachers ought prudently to enforce upon our members the necessity of teaching their slaves to read the Word of God; and also that they give them time to hear the Word of God preached on our regular days of divine service.

" *Resolved,* 2. That our colored preachers and official members have all the privileges in the district and quarterly-meeting conferences which the usages of the country, in different sections, will justify : *Provided*, also, that the presiding elder may, when there is a sufficient number, hold for them a separate district conference.

"*Resolved*, 3. That any of the annual conferences may employ colored preachers to travel where they judge their services necessary : *Provided*, they be recommended according to the form of Discipline.

"*Resolved*, 4. That the above resolutions be made a part of the section in the Discipline on slavery."

Since nothing aside from the action already taken by the Church on this subject was done until the year 1836, when the General Conference met for its twelfth session in Cincinnati, Ohio, we pass from the General Conference of 1824 to the General Conference of 1836. The agitation of this question went steadily on, however, and the Abolitionists kept it warm. From Maine to Louisiana, from Canada to Florida, it was being agitated. Since so much was said concerning the question at that General Conference, some of which, if not retrogression, was akin to it, we give the following resolutions. In reading the same, and judging them, we must remember that the seeming opposition to Abolitionism was attributable, in a measure, to the aversion to politics; that the tide of agitation was even then so high that the strongest of strong men

MORGAN COLLEGE, BALTIMORE, MD.

trembled; that the Church had time and again put itself on record as to the question at issue. Though it, for the time being, condemned the action of the two "lecturing delegates," it never once relaxed its grip upon the throat of slavery, nor assayed to compromise a single principle of right. So far removed from the scenes that greeted the General Conference that year in Cincinnati, and remembering how thoughtless some advocates of measures can sometimes be or appear, and how easily a zeal without knowledge can injure a good cause, we do not wonder at the action taken in the case of those two brethren. But when the enemies of human liberty construed the condemnation of the action of those two brethren by the General Conference as a weakening by the Church on the question of slavery, the ensuing General Conference disabused their minds of their error, and sent the enemies of liberty to grass again.

The following are the resolutions above referred to, enacted by the *General Conference of 1836:*

"WHEREAS, Great excitement has prevailed in this country on the subject of modern Abolitionism, which is reported to have been increased in this city recently by the unjustifiable conduct of two members of the General Conference in lecturing upon and in favor of that agitating topic; and WHEREAS, such a course on the part of any of its members is calculated to bring upon this body the suspicions and distrust of the community, and misrepresent its sentiments in regard to the point at issue; and WHEREAS, in this aspect of the case, a due regard for its own character, as well as a just concern for the interests of the Church confided to its care, demand a full, decided, and unequivocal expression of the views of the General Conference in the premises; therefore,

"*Resolved*, by the delegates of the annual conferences, in General Conference assembled, That they disapprove, in the most unqualified sense, the conduct of two members of the General Conference, who are reported to have lectured in this city, recently, upon and in favor of modern Abolitionism.

"2. That they are decidedly opposed to modern Abolitionism, and wholly disclaim any right, wish, or intention to interfere in the civil and political relation between master and slave, as it exists in the slaveholding States of this Union.

"3. That the foregoing preamble and resolutions be published in our periodicals."

The report of the Judiciary Committee is here given also, touching this question at another point:

"The Judiciary Committee, to whom was referred the petition of the official members of the Methodist Episcopal Church on Lancaster Circuit, Baltimore Conference, report, that the petition referred to them is an able document, drawn up in the most respectful language, and signed by twenty-nine individuals, who claimed to be official members of the Methodist Episcopal Church on Lancaster Circuit.

"The petitioners first invite the attention of the General Conference to the section of the Discipline which states that 'no slaveholder shall be eligible to any official station in our Church hereafter, when the laws of the State in which he lives will admit of emancipation, and permit the liberated slave to enjoy freedom,' etc. They then produce an extract of the laws from the commonwealth of Virginia, showing their extreme rigor in this matter, 'That any emancipated slave (with exceptions too rare to be looked for in one case out of many) remaining in the commonwealth more than twelve months after his or her right to freedom shall have arrived, contrary to the provisions of this act, shall be sold by the overseers of the poor, in any county in which he or she may be found, for the benefit of the literary fund.' In view of this act they claim that they, as official members, are protected by the Discipline of the Church, as they deem it to be precisely one of the exceptions to the General Rule provided for in the Discipline; and especially as under the existing laws of the commonwealth to emancipate their slaves would, in many cases, be an act of cruelty to the slaves themselves. The matter of complaint by the petitioners is, that the construction put upon this rule by the Baltimore Annual Conference, in certain acts respecting individuals connected with this section of the work, is subversive of their rights and oppressive in its bearings; that they require the same submission to the rule of persons in that State as of those in sections where the legal disability to comply with it does not exist, regardless of the exceptions. And they respectfully solicit the interference of the General Conference, either to revise the rule, or give it such construction as to afford them relief in the premises; or, finally, if neither be done, to cause them to be set off to the Virginia Conference.

"It is due to the Baltimore Conference to say that the cases referred to as evidence of their improper application of their rule, are stated in terms too vague and indefinite to authorize the inference drawn by the petitioners. It is represented that a young man applying to be received into the itinerancy is prevented by application of this rule; that it is in vain for him to urge upon a majority of the conference the impracticability of his complying with the rule, in consequence of the laws under which he lives, or any other consideration in favor of his being received; because he will not comply with the rule, he must be rejected. The same, it is assumed by the petitioners, is done with respect to those who apply for ordination. And it is inferred by them, that if the conference act consistently, stewards and leaders may be expected soon to be called upon to comply with the rule, or forfeit their official standing in the Church.

"Your committee view this subject in a very different light. In admitting a preacher to travel, or electing one to orders, a conference must have the right to act freely; and in cases which are not successful, it is wholly an assumption, on the part of the applicants or their friends, to say what particular considerations dictated the vote, unless such considerations be distinctly avowed by a majority of the conference. And it is known to all conversant with the transactions of an annual conference, that no person applying to be received or ordained ever enters as a party before the conference, pleading his own cause, and hearing and answering the objections which may be urged against his application. Any act of conference, then, in these cases, can not be justly urged as evidence that the conference denies the party concerned the benefit of the special provision in the rule. A conference or other deliberative bodies possess, and in the nature of the case must possess, the right to determine its own course, and vote freely in all such individual cases. Your committee, therefore, can not see that the privileges claimed by the petitioners have been contravened by an act of the Baltimore Conference.

"Having said this much respecting the alleged grounds of grievance, your committee agree in the opinion that the exceptions to the General Rule in the Discipline, referred to by the petitioners, clearly apply to official members of the Church in Virginia, according to the laws of the commonwealth, and do therefore protect them against a forfeiture of their official standing on account of said rule. In addition to the petition of the official members of Lancaster Circuit, a resolution of a quarterly conference of Westmoreland Circuit has been referred to your committee, by which it appears that the members of said conference concurred in said petition. Should the General Conference agree in the opinions stated by the committee in the report, it is respectfully recommended that, after adopting it, they cause a copy of it to be forwarded to the official members in each of the above-named circuits. All of which is respectfully submitted.

"The committee to whom were referred sundry memorials from the North, praying that certain rules on the subject of slavery, which formerly existed in our book of Discipline, should be restored, and that the General Conference take such measures as they may deem proper to free the Church from the evil of slavery, beg leave to report:

"That they have had the subject under serious consideration, and are of opinion that the prayers of the memorialists can not be granted, believing that it would be highly improper for the General Conference to take any action that would alter or change our rules on the subject of slavery. Your committee, therefore, respectfully submit the following resolution:

"*Resolved*, etc., That'it is inexpedient to make any change in our book of Discipline respecting slavery; and that we deem it improper further to agitate the subject in the General Conference at present.

"All of which is respectfully submitted."

The pastoral address presented to and accepted by that General Conference, at once puts forever at rest any shadow of a doubt as to any disposition of the Church to compromise with slavery. We quote the closing part touching this question, viz:

"It can not be unknown to you that the question of slavery in these United States, by the constitutional compact which binds us together as a nation, is left to be regulated by the several State Legislatures themselves, and thereby is put beyond the control of the General Government, as well as that of all ecclesiastical bodies; it being manifest that in the slaveholding States themselves the entire responsibility of its existence or non-existence rests with those State Legislatures. And such is the aspect of affairs in reference to this question, that whatever else might tend to ameliorate the condition of the slave, it is evident to us, from what we have witnessed of Abolition movements, that these are the least likely to do him good. On the contrary, we have it in evidence before us that the inflammatory speeches and writings and movements have tended, in many instances, injuriously to affect his temporal and spiritual condition by hedging up the way of the missionary who is sent to preach to him Jesus and the resurrection, and by making a more rigid supervision necessary on the part of his overseer, thereby abridging his civil and religious liberties."

General Conference of 1840.—Test cases touching slavery were continually arising. That of Silas Comfort was among the most noted. No one will, for a moment, deny that this noted case was as complicated as noted, and was, we believe, on the whole as we now see it, settled for the best interests of the Church and the colored race. The decision was not what could have been expected; but, then, "discretion is the better part of valor." There were, of course, two sides—two separate and distinct parties concerned. While the interests of a class within the Methodist Episcopal Church were at stake, the unity and tranquillity of the Church were on the altar. The action of Rev. Silas Comfort was an entering wedge between the two parties within the Church. Many earnest, honest men thought it a strange procedure when that General Conference declared it "inexpedient and unjustifiable for any preacher among us to permit colored persons to give testimony against white persons in any State where they are denied that privilege in trials at law." This was passed by a vote of 74 to 46. Twenty-two members of that General Conference did not vote at all. Whether the spirit that gave birth to the Wesleyan Methodist Church three years afterward kept them from voting, is not recorded. Whether that decision hastened the organization of the above-mentioned Church or not, many believe it did. The decision, since in it the word "denied" appears, was probably the best the

General Conference thought it could do under existing circumstances, coupled with the restriction to those "States where they are denied that privilege in trials at law." The reason for rendering such a decision probably rested upon the fact that otherwise it might have led to internal wranglings in the general Church, and imposed additional hardships upon the colored man, in that masters would probably have felt it incumbent upon themselves to prohibit any slave from enjoying the benefits derivable from membership in the Methodist Episcopal Church, and thus added injury to insult, and left them a prey to "the false accuser of the brethren." Notwithstanding the construction others put upon that decision, or what we now think of it, the colored members of the Methodist Episcopal Church were not well pleased, as a protest from Sharp Street Church declares. The author of "The Anti-slavery Struggle and Triumph in the Methodist Episcopal Church," at page 148, says: "At the General Conference of 1840 a memorial was prepared by forty official members of Sharp Street and Asbury Churches, in Baltimore, protesting against the colored-testimony resolution. It was put in the hands of Rev. Thomas B. Sargent, and by him given to one of the bishops. Through the efforts of Dr. Bond and others the memorialists were pacified without the conference knowing anything of the document." The Rev. Dr. Elliott declared that "the colored members of the Church were greatly afflicted. This matter had like to have done great mischief." The document was afterward published. Among other things equally pungent, the memorialists said:

"We have learned with profound regret and unutterable emotion of the resolution adopted May 18th, which has inflicted, we fear, an irreparable injury upon eighty thousand souls for whom Christ died; souls which, by this act of your venerable body, have been stripped of the dignity of Christians, degraded in the scale of humanity, and treated as criminals, for no other reason than the color of their skin. The adoption of this soul-sickening resolution has destroyed the peace and alienated the affections of twenty-five hundred members of the Church in this city, who now feel that they are but spiritual orphans or scattered sheep. The deed you have done could not have originated in that love which works no ill to his neighbor, but in a disposition to propitiate that spirit which is not to be appeased, except through concessions derogatory to the dignity of our holy religion! And, therefore, they protest against it, and conjure you to wipe from the journal the odious resolution."

This was strong language, prompted by a stronger feeling.

The members of Sharp Street Church did not protest against the decision of the Church in this case, because they doubted the expressed fidelity made prior to this, that was self-evident. But they knew that times change and men change with them. This to them looked like a compromise with the spirit of slavery that stalked abroad in the land. That decision, viewed from this distance to-day, to some, assumes a different aspect altogether. How could they keep from protesting? What could they do more, how dare do less? How did they curb their feelings enough to express their thoughts in such mild language? Why should not those burden-bound colored men and women protest against, while compelled to submit to, a decision that to them was humiliating in the extreme? Shall the crawling, loathsome worm of the dust be allowed to squirm when trod upon, the venomous snake to hiss, the vicious beast to defend himself, and then deny the right to protest? Could the Church of God deny them the privilege of exculpating themselves in the eyes of the public from what to them appeared an undeserved reproach, thrown upon them because of their color or helpless condition, casting thereby away from them the protection of all save that of God? As they probably thought, why thus insult them? Aye; rather why insult justice and God by demanding of them a reason for protesting, since it appeared to them that the Methodist Episcopal Church—the Church, and only Church, that from the beginning had stood manfully in their defense—by that decision "had failed to manifest the spirit that worketh no ill to its neighbor?" Whatever the protestants in this instance may have thought or said, viewed at that time from the *ignis fatuus* of the then existing African Churches in the North, "it was calculated to drive out of the Methodist Episcopal Church every intelligent and manly colored man," into one or the other of these Churches. Viewed, however, under the light of the Address of our bishops at that time, it assumes a more rational and philosophical aspect. The bishops said: "We can not withhold from you at this eventful period the solemn conviction of our minds, that no ecclesiastical legislation on the subject of slavery at this time will have a tendency to accomplish these most desirable objects, to wit: Preserve the peace and unity of the whole body, promote the greatest happiness of the slave population, and advance generally in the slaveholding community of our country the humane and hallowing influence of our holy religion." By this we judge that at that time the Church had come to the conclusion that it was impossible by "ecclesiastical legislation" to benefit in any way the colored man; that extra legislation on the question would be not only supererogatory, but in all probability only beneficial in goading the slaveholder. We infer (1) that civil legislation touching slavery was not objected to; but that (2) the objection to the admission of colored testimony had been raised by the civil courts, and it was not considered being "subject to the powers that be" to demur; at least, that it was the duty of the Church "to

live in peace with all men" as much as possible.
We are not ignorant of the fact that there have
been, and will yet be, times when forbearance
ceases to be a virtue, and when the Church of God
can not afford to be loyal "to the powers that be."
But what could be accomplished by the opposition of *one Church* to the slave oligarchy that
was then rife in this country? As to this we can
only say :

> "Deep in unfathomable mines
>   Of never-failing skill,
>   God treasures up his bright designs,
>   And works his sovereign will."

As we now see it, there was no use for Methodism to push slavery harder at that time, since God
was behind the movement. Long before this time
the bishops and other far-seeing and right-minded
men saw that all the speeches made and actions
taken pro and con relating to slavery, by the
Church, would, without the interposition of God,
culminate in splitting the Church. This in itself
gave promise of what actually grew out of it—a long,
bitter, but bloodless ecclesiastical war between the
two factions. Seeing signs of an approaching crisis,
they were anxious to avert it as long as possible,
and at the same time prayed to God, "Thy will be
done, and not mine;" that when the on-sweeping tidal
wave, even then within the bounds of the Church,
in opposition to holding slaves, did come, that, so far
as those who were leading in opposition to the

accursed traffic were concerned, their consciences might be clear, and that if the separation came in their life-time, their side should bear the marks of God's approbation.

Without multiplying evidence going to show the interest the Methodist Episcopal Church took in the colored man from its origin to the time at which we have arrived, we wish now to note the result of the unwillingness of the Church to compromise with slavery. We have seen that in every case where it was possible to make concessions to the colored man, to train, protect, and elevate him, the Church has done it where it was proper and best for him. It has in every case, as far as practicable, tried to remedy the wrongs perpetrated upon him as well as lessen his burdens. Not, of course, always as the colored man thought it ought to have been done—for he was not in condition to even judge what was best for him—nor yet as some who appeared more radical would have had it done; but the Church stood by and for the colored man as no other denomination occupying the same territory and similar circumstances would do. To know what was contemplated by the Church in this case we have but to trace out the legitimate results. During the interregnum from 1836 to 1844 "God moved in a mysterious way his wonders to perform." The question of the abolition of American slavery was discussed at each General Conference with animation and seriousness. Many declared the radical action taken by the Church on the question would eventually rend the Church in twain. Many earnest prayers ascended to the throne of God in behalf of the tranquillity of the Church, but were not answered because "his brother" was in need; and those prayers, if answered, would not only have riveted his shackles, but bathed his face in tears, and consigned the poor colored man and his posterity, not to perpetual banishment—that would have been tolerable—but to a slavery worse than that of the Russian serf. As many more prayed that the prediction as to the split in the Church might come to pass. As a result, each succeeding General Conference was marked by the friends of slavery as the beginning of the end of a united Methodism in America.

CHAPTER III.

THE CRISIS—ITS CAUSE.

THE General Conference of 1844 sat in the city of New York, from May 1st until June 10th—forty-five days. It has gone down into history as the most noted of any General Conference of the Church. There was at stake the peace, unity, and strength of Methodism in this country. The question most prominent, and that was calculated to stir up most enthusiasm, was that of the abolition of American slavery. An unprecedented, as well as strange case, came up for consideration. Rev. James Osgood Andrew, one of the bishops of the Methodist Episcopal Church, who was elected at the General Conference of 1832, a few months before the session of the General Conference of 1844 had married an estimable lady of the best families of Georgia, who was the owner of slaves. This act on the part of the bishop, from the very nature of things, caused much excitement and more comment. This was a trying attitude for the Church. There had arisen within a party in the North that accused it of being pro-slavery in sentiment—at least to a certain extent. Notwithstanding it hitherto had occupied such strong positions on the question of human slavery, the above sentiment arose to such a height in 1842 as to cause a secession, and the formation of the Wesleyan Methodist Church. It did, therefore, seem strange that such a thing had happened.

But now it appeared as if the crisis had been reached. Just what action that General Conference could or would take now on the question of slavery in general, and the bishop's case in particular, was hard to imagine. The natural supposition with the Abolitionists was that the same vituperation and obloquy would be manifested against slavery as of yore; that the rules relating to slavery would be adhered to, even where it involved a popular bishop of that Church. It was a trying situation. Others declared it impracticable and irrational for the great Methodist Episcopal Church to interfere with the personal rights of the bishop by declaring that he was in the wrong, when he did not claim the slaves as his property. Some declared the Church would now back down, and thus verify the allegations of the Wesleyan brethren. If it had not been for the confidence the Church had in the bishop, and in many others who professed to believe slavery right, they could easily have concluded that a trap had been set to catch the General Conference, because the bishop was not the only one involved. A member of the Baltimore Annual Conference had also, by marriage, become a slaveholder and refused to manumit his slaves. In the State of Maryland emancipation was possible. After the Baltimore Conference had carefully considered his case, he was suspended from the ministry of the Church. He appealed from the decision of his conference to the ensuing General Conference. When the case came up on the appeal, the decision of the lower court was sustained by a large majority. In the meantime the Committee on Episcopacy waited upon Bishop Andrew. He informed the committee that he had married a wife who inherited slaves from her former husband; that her husband had secured them to her by a deed of trust; and that she could not emancipate them if she desired to do so. The committee, however, aware of the fact that it was possible for the bishop to remove from the State of Georgia where emancipation was not possible, to a State where it was possible, took the case under consideration.

Here were two factions—one in favor of standing up for the emancipation of slaves, supported by thousands of influential Northern and Eastern men and money; the other, supported by not less than fifty thousand members, institutions of learning, and the slaveholding States and slaveholding sympathizers from the Atlantic to the great West, from the Lakes to the Gulf, and every slaveholding country in the entire world. Speeches, noting these facts, and declaring a bitter unwillingness to crouch before the spirit of freedom, manifested by that part of the Church which opposed the holding of slaves, began to make a breach in the Church that eternity alone, we fear, can only close. The Board of Bishops were divided on the question. From North to South, from East to West, the Church of God was disturbed. Not only this, but the world knew that if the Methodist Episcopal Church split then and there on that question, and any respectable portion opposed slavery, it would be the beginning of the end of slavery on American soil. Therefore, even the political and mercantile worlds were anxiously waiting, as well as earnestly working, either to reconcile the affair or compromise it. Any way in the world not to divide on *that question at that time.* God only knows how many colored people in this country sent up prayers from the rice-swamps of the Carolinas, the cotton-fields of Mississippi, and the cane-brakes of Louisiana, that "the God of Elijah, who answered prayer by fire," would bow the gentle heavens and visit New York City with a baptism of the Holy Ghost, that that General Conference—the men of God therein—might have victory in favor of the Church, suffering humanity, and God. If there was ever any time at which more prayers besieged the throne of grace than another, it surely must have been during the General Conference of the Methodist Episcopal Church in 1844. It is not an exaggeration to say the eyes and ears of the world were turned toward that General Conference. And why not? Were not even then the interests of every Methodist in the known world, of every colored man, woman, and

child, and children of the race then in the womb
of the future—aye, the future destiny of him who
pens these lines, with that of our holy Christian
religion at stake?   Most assuredly it was so.

Some declared that Bishop Andrew would have
willingly yielded to the opinions of the General
Conference had not his brethren in the slaveholding States and others persuaded him that it was his
duty to stand by them on this question, involving
their personal rights.   While we do not stop to
express a doubt as to whether, indeed, this was uppermost in his mind, we are glad to note that, notwithstanding the interests at stake, and that the
Church at that time could have saved itself much
trouble, filled its coffers with "golden ducats,"
increased its popularity, and the sound of its ap-
plause would have resounded on earth from sea to
sea and from shore to shore, after a protracted
discussion, that General Conference, by a vote of
110 to 68,

"*Resolved*, That it is the sense of this General
Conference that he [Bishop Andrew] desist from
the exercise of his office so long as this impediment
remains."

At this action the Southern conferences felt
deeply aggrieved.   A clap of thunder from a clear
sky could not have spread greater consternation
and excited more feeling than did this action.
Like wildfire the news began to spread.   So far as
the United States mails could carry it, the news

was spread before a fortnight. What was to be the outcome but few hesitated to say. What could it be but that which had been repeatedly predicted, the separation of the Southern conferences from the Methodist Episcopal Church?

At once meetings were called by the Southern delegates, and steps were taken looking to the organization of a Church in the South. The following year the organization was accomplished, showing that the matter had been thoroughly canvassed, and a conclusion reached by the slaveholding element that was not to be surrendered. Is he a philosopher who sees in this a counterpart to the drama of Pharaoh and the Hebrews? Is it not possible to trace the finger-marks of Providence all along the pages of every resolution offered by the Methodist Episcopal Church on this question from 1796 to date? Does not it appear in all this that our God,

> "Deep in unfathomable mines
>   Of never-failing skill,
> Treasures up his bright designs
>   And works his sovereign will?"

The chief part of the membership in the entire slaveholding territory, with the exception of the States of Maryland and Delaware, separated and formed the Methodist Episcopal Church, South. The grand old Methodist Church, by adhering to her anti-slavery principles in this particular case, lost nearly five hundred thousand members, the

control of much Church property, and many institutions of learning; incurring thereby the ill-will,
everywhere, of every man, woman, and child who
was pro-slavery in theory or practice. But what
effect had this action of the Church on the minds of
the colored people? Did they really believe it meant
what the pro-slavery element declared it meant,
that the Methodist Episcopal Church was an inveterate enemy to what Wesley called "the sum of
all villainies?" Any one who doubts the fact that
the colored man everywhere, who was capable of
properly appreciating philanthropy, appreciated the
situation, has but to note the fact that, comparatively, the States of Maryland, Delaware, Louisiana,
Mississippi, and South Carolina, so far as Methodism among our people is concerned, *belong to the
Methodist Episcopal Church;* some of the most intelligent colored men of the Church are there.
The saying, "It is an ill wind that blows nobody
good," was verified in this instance. The colored
membership within the Church renewed its resolutions, redoubled its diligence, and had its faith
strengthened in the integrity of Methodism. They
recognized in the Church a mother whose tender
solicitude and maternal care were not based upon
anticipated future benefits derivable from the colored membership, but, commensurate with their
integrity and Christianity, she expected to help
them; that she was a mother who not only labored
to have them "flee from the wrath to come," but to

save them, as well, from the rigorous burdens of the unrequited toil of slavery; that she was a mother who loved them for Jesus' sake, and stood by them when it was neither profitable nor pleasant to do so. A new inspiration seems to have come to the entire Church. But was not that to have been expected as a matter of course, under the command with promise, "Bring ye all the tithes into the storehouse, and prove me herewith, saith the Lord of hosts, if I will not open you the windows of heaven, and pour you out a blessing, that there shall not be room enough to receive it. And all nations shall call you blessed." Had not the Church planted itself upon the Ten Commandments—the rock of ages; and was there not to be seen everywhere the bright, shining light from the Sermon on the Mount athwart the path of the Church in its onward march in favor of the recognition among all men, of whatever complexion, of the wholesome doctrine and practice of the common Fatherhood of God and the brotherhood of man? As a result, that part of the Methodist Episcopal Church that believed it better to obey God than man, to be unpopular and sneered at, but right; that "bore unmoved the world's dread frown, nor heeded its scornful smile," received a new baptism of the Holy Ghost, and continued receiving it until *a new door was opened unto the Church.*

Notwithstanding the fact that nearly five hundred thousand members left the Church on account of the decision on slavery, by no means all left who wished the colored man would leave or be forced out of the Church into one of the two colored organizations. It may as well be said now, that there has always been a faction within and without the Church that has used, or attempted to use, the colored man in opposition to the Methodist Episcopal Church. In the first place, they use him as a wedge. When they are foiled in an attempt to carry any certain thing, they at once declare that the Methodist Episcopal Church has been, and is now, taking advantage of the poor colored man. If this does not answer, they find it convenient to let him (the colored man) understand that he is an intruder in the Church, and respect for his manhood demands that he go out and "paddle his own canoe;" that white men will think more of him if he exhibit "the self-reliance and ability displayed by those members who are in separate Churches to themselves." When this proved abortive, they found it convenient to demonstrate it. They at once invited some minister of one of the two colored organizations to occupy their (white) pulpits, and leave the colored minister within our Church without such invitation. The result was almost inevitable. Pretty soon the more manly members of our Church, in the community where such tricks were played, would begin to say : " Well, that's passing strange, that white ministers of our Church prefer African ministers to our own. It must be because of their independence. If that's so, we want some of it also." That an undercurrent of this kind has flowed along the stream of Methodism ever since the colored membership question has been discussed, is easily proven. Now the class of which we have just spoken is to be distinguished from the class who honestly believed that it would be better for the white and the colored members to be separate. Not that they (the whites spoken of) were unwilling to aid the colored members, nor yet because they did not want them saved, but because the loud professions and *announced* success of the separate colored organizations blinded their eyes. These considered, and rightly so too, all such persons their best allies. The African and African Zion Churches whispered continually, and sometimes preached, that the colored membership in the Methodist Episcopal Church was a burden to the white folks. These organizations, though supported by some within our Church, saw there were but two ways in which they could induce the colored element in the Methodist Episcopal Church to join them,—by loud professions of "race pride," and appeals to their ignorance and prejudice. This they attempted by appeals to the dignity of our colored local preachers; by telling the more ignorant that they were being imposed upon by "white folks." They told the local preachers, class-leaders, etc., among our members, that it was a shame for them to have white masters during the week and white masters on the Sabbath-day also; that they were as well qualified literarily to have charge of congregations with white members as some of the white pastors; that they possessed intelligence enough to do business for themselves. Then, again, they would say: "There will never come a time when the Methodist Episcopal Church will allow one of you colored members to preside as their presiding elder or pastor; that all the property you buy belongs to 'white folks,' and not to you."

The language of their most accurate historian will give a faint idea of the pressure we speak of, which was and is now brought to bear upon our people in some localities. He says: "It is true our colored brethren within the communion of the Methodist Episcopal Church worship in a large number of churches in Maryland, Delaware, and other of the Southern States, and many of them are fine ones; but the question is: 'To whom do they belong—the congregations worshiping in them, or the Methodist Episcopal Church?' We all know that it is our glory, that our churches belong to no one congregation or body of trustees in particular, but to the connection in general." Again, *ibid:* "It would have been a source of unspeakable joy had he been able or permitted truthfully to record that your Church had acknowledged your full and true manhood, and not denied it both in practice and in law; that it had opened its school-doors to you, as did other Christian bodies, and like them, too, have received you into conference upon a perfect ministerial equality; but, alas! the doors of its schools, and of its conferences as well, were locked, and bolted, and barred against you." He was quoting and commenting upon the words of another. Such strong talk, mixed as it was with braggadocio, pretty soon had the desired effect upon two large classes amongst us—the ambitious illiterates and the pompous, aspiring for recognition, minus merit. These two classes were soon, after such a process of pumping, inflated until their sides puffed nearly to bursting. A number of the above-mentioned classes soon concluded that they must be in a Church where there was a favorable chance for every member of an annual conference to be put forth before the world as a noted preacher, appointed presiding elder or a General Conference officer, or elected to the bishopric. It is difficult for any one, who understands in some sort the feelings of white men when they are ambitious for notoriety or office and fail, to say or appreciate the feelings of a disappointed colored man who has known nothing save ostracism. To expect him to refuse preferment, emolument, or office, when tendered, is to expect an ox in August to refuse the shade. Notwithstanding the disadvantages the colored man has labored under hitherto, he has found out that in a nation of blind men the one-eyed man ought to be, and is, king. To this day but few white people have learned that it is not always the most profitable thing to exchange an old lamp for a new one; that "it is better to bear the ills we have, than fly to others we know not of."

To say that at no time a single colored member within the Methodist Episcopal Church imagined the wool was being pulled over his eyes by men of lighter hue, is going too far. To say there never was a white man in the Methodist Episcopal Church who refused to recognize or affiliate with the colored members because of their color, who refused to do for him there what he would have done if he had been elsewhere, or had been "manly and independent like some others, and paddled his own canoe," or that all such have left the Methodist Episcopal Church, is going farther than truth warrants or the case requires. To say that any organization among men is absolutely perfect, is preposterous; for even the Methodist Episcopal Church in this country is not what it can and will be. I fear much of the unrest, and seventy-five per cent of the withdrawals of our colored membership since 1812, could directly or indirectly be attributed to the actions of those within and without the Church who think more of caste than Christ, more of popularity than right, and more of men's opinions than of God's Word. Notwithstanding this, we hazard the statement that, during that time, there has not been an hour when the heart of Methodism in general, and the Methodist Episcopal Church in particular, did not beat in unison with that of the Christ of God, the blessed Master, who, in the midst of a gainsaying world, said: "I call you not servants, for the servant knoweth not what his Lord doeth; but I called you brethren." And yet, in nearly every instance of attack made by the two colored organizations upon the colored members in our Church up to this time, and for that matter all time, the exceptions among our white and colored membership have by them been spoken of as the rule. Their statements as to the intelligence or ignorance of our colored membership was the natural if not legitimate outgrowth of the disposition, action, and words of some of our white members who remain in, but were not in spirit of the Methodist Episcopal Church. This is true of some of the ministers as well as white members of our Church. When the bishops, General Conference officers, pastors, or members of the two colored organizations visited communities where we had churches, *they were welcomed as no other colored Methodists were*, if for no other than for the reason that they were high in authority within their own Church. This distinction was not always clear in the minds of our members. There is no doubt that this caused us much trouble as well as loss of preachers and lay members. In those States where our membership was the largest and most influential, and where our churches were better and finer, the effects of such stuff were more telling because of the spirit of the people. Our members saw at once that one of three things had to be done to hold our members: a complete colored organization had to be formed among us; or else join with the one or the other of those organizations; or else have separate annual conferences within our Church, so that the presiding elderate, pastorate, trusteeship, and stewardship would be in the hands and charge of our colored members.

It was not in the mind of the two eagles that stirred up this nest, that matters would turn out as they did—that instead of an exode from the mother of Methodism into the bosom of the daughter, a separate perch could and would be prepared. The anticipation was that all the colored members in the Church would flock into the two African Churches. This hope kept those two organizations from uniting, while each thought its numbers would soon be increased by the coming of the colored members from our Church. The more intelligent colored men in our Church saw and felt that something *had to be done*, and done quickly. I could wish they had opened their eyes sooner. Those two organizations knew well enough that if the colored members within the Methodist Episcopal Church in the North, East, and the States bordering on the above sections decided to leave, one or the other, or both of these, would get them. There was no other Church into which they could go. Hence they worked and faithfully watched every movement of our Church touching the colored people. They well knew that if all the colored members in the Methodist Episcopal Church joined in a body either one of their organizations, the result would be one great, grand colored Methodist Church. I truly believe the good men in the Methodist Episcopal Church, among which we put our bishops, saw it in that light. I believe other white members in our Church were laboring every day for the sole object of bringing about a union of all the colored Methodists. They believed that the colored man had been a source of annoyance; that the good brethren who left the Church in 1844 would return if the colored members all left the Methodist Episcopal Church; that it would be a great set-back as well as rebuke to the "hot-headed Abolitionists" who kept it in an uproar about the colored man, and would prove conclusively that the radical element within it was all wrong and the conservative element was all right.

When the General Conference of 1848 met in the city of Pittsburg, several petitions from the colored members of our Church in Pennsylvania, Delaware, and Maryland were presented. The petitioners asked that, since the Church had ordained colored ministers, they be given the charge of the congregations over which white pastors had presided; that a separate conference be granted them within the Methodist Episcopal Church. These petitions were not only received, but respectfully and carefully considered. The petitions were properly and promptly referred to the Committee on the State of the Church. In due time the above named committee reported as follows:

"We find among the papers presented for our consideration memorials from different places within the slave States from our colored membership, praying for recognition, in that colored ministers be sent to them; for the organization and manning of districts; and that they be granted a separate annual conference,—which memorials are signed by 2,735 members."

Thus it is clearly seen that much unrest was caused by the delay on the part of our Church in granting a separate conference. Our work to-day would have been as strong, comparatively, in the Eastern and Northern States as either of the African Churches, had it not been for the delay in granting us a separate conference. As a result nearly all the colored members of our Church in the North and East were persuaded to unite with one or the other of the African Churches which were under the fostering care in some way of our Church, while they desperately fought the colored element within it. Of course, this is strange. A fact remains, that the great Methodist Episcopal Church felt that while under obligations to help the colored man, and more able to do so than others, she was unwilling to have him *driven* away, whether by centrifugal or centripetal force. The committee above referred to continued its report as follows:

" We recommend the following :

" *Resolved,* That we recognize all persons in these United States, who were members of the Methodist Episcopal Church in 1844, who have not separated from said Church by withdrawals or expulsion according to the Discipline of the Church, and who express a desire to be recognized as under our care and jurisdiction, as members of the Methodist Episcopal Church ; and that we regard it our duty, as far as practicable, to supply all such with the preaching and ordinances of the gospel."

The special report in this case on the petition from the Sharpe Street Church of Baltimore, asking for a separate conference, reported as follows :

"That having carefully considered the memorials, and feeling an earnest desire to do all that can be done to promote the spiritual interests of our colored people, they recommend to the General Conference for adoption the following resolutions:

" *Resolved,* That the organization of such (separate) conferences at present is inexpedient.

" *Resolved,* That the Discipline be so amended that the fifth answer in section 10, part 2, shall read as follows: 'The bishops may employ colored preachers to travel and preach where their services are judged necessary: *Provided,* that no one shall be so employed without having been recommended by a quarterly conference.'"

Thus the work of the colored members of the

Methodist Episcopal Church began as the great Church itself began, evolving out of necessity, and guided by Providence.

The already existing Churches—the African and African Zion—were not allowed to operate to any great extent in the Southern States by the customs and laws of these States; hence, without giving any reason, it was wise to conclude that at that time, and in that territory, the organization of a separate colored conference among our people, within the Church, was "inexpedient." And yet the Church was willing to do what it thought best under existing circumstances. The colored ministers within the Church were henceforth to travel and preach at the discretion of the bishops. This was the beginning of colored traveling preachers in the Methodist Episcopal Church.

CHAPTER IV.

THE COLORED PASTORATE.

THE employment of colored ministers in the traveling connection in the Church, like Methodism itself, was a child of necessity. It has grown to be a man, however, and is the father of several children. Notwithstanding the secession of nearly all our white conferences and Churches—500,000 members in the slaveholding States before mentioned—the record is not written where the Methodist Episcopal Church extended overtures to them to return that in any way involved the relinquishment of its hold on the throat of slavery, or that equaled that offered by our revered president, Abraham Lincoln, to the Southern Confederacy, if they would return to the Union. The whole question of opposing slavery by the Church seems to have been, all along, a work of conscience. not to be repented of; that the work had to be done, because the seal of God's approval rested upon it. The action and firm stand taken by the Church in 1844 put a quietus upon all who professed to believe the rules relating to slavery. would not be enforced during the ensuing quadrennium.

The General Conference of 1852, that met in the city of Boston, was called upon to consider the expediency of separate conferences for colored members. The custom of the Church had usually been to leave all colored congregations, in the appointments, "to be supplied." But as the work progressed and the colored membership found the braggadocio of those "who went out from us" was invading the rank and file of their work; that each year it increased with telling and disheartening effect, and the more ambitious members among us were becoming restless and wavering in their opinions, threatening with dissolution the work of the colored members within the Church, the members within the bounds of the Philadelphia and New Jersey Conferences—at any rate from members of our Church in Pennsylvania and New Jersey—sent up, not only memorials to this General Conference, but representative men of the more intelligent class, to represent them and see, at the same time, the way the great Methodist Episcopal Church would treat colored memorialists. When the memorials were presented, asking again for separate conferences, they were promptly referred to the Committee on Missions. After careful·examination of the memorials, they called before them the representatives. "An open and free discussion of the interests at stake and the benefits anticipated therefrom, was had." The committee then submitted to the General Conference the following:

"The Committee on Missions, to whom was referred the petition of our colored brethren from Philadelphia, asking that the pastors within the

Philadelphia and New Jersey Annual Conferences may be formed into an annual conference, under the supervision of the bishops and of the presiding elders of said conference within whose bounds their (the colored pastors') work may lie, beg leave to report that the committee have given due consideration to the petition, and have heard the bearers of it in person, and have obtained all the information within their reach, and have come to the following conclusions:

"1. That it is very desirable that the colored pastors mentioned in the petition aforesaid should have an opportunity to meet together once a year, in the presence, or under the supervision, of the bishop or bishops, in order to confer together with respect to the best means of promoting their work, and to receive the assignment of their work from the bishops to the Churches usually left in the Minutes 'to be supplied.'

"2. That in this meeting it is desirable that the presiding elders, in whose bounds the colored Churches and congregations lie, should be present to assist the bishop in the assignment of the work.

"3. *Provided*, upon due inquiry by the bishops, they shall find a sufficient number of colored preachers of sufficient qualifications to justify an annual meeting. Having arrived at these conclusions, the committee have agreed on the following resolution, which is reported for adoption by this General Conference:

"*Resolved*, That we advise that the colored local

preachers now employed, or who may be employed, within the bounds of the Philadelphia and New Jersey Annual Conferences, be assembled together once in each year by the bishop or bishops, who may preside in said conference, for the purpose of conferring with the said colored local preachers with respect to the best means for promoting their work, and also for the purpose of assigning their work, respectively; and that the presiding elders within whose bounds and under whose care the colored Churches and congregations are, be present and aid the bishop or bishops in said annual meeting of local preachers: *Provided*, that upon due inquiry the said bishop or bishops shall find such annual meeting aforesaid to be practicable and expedient."

So far as we have gone, we have seen a disposition on the part of the Church to give the colored man all the rights and benefits practicable and wise that are accorded other members. It was not to have been expected that he would demand what was not best for him as he saw it, or that he should be given what he asked for when it was as impracticable as unwise. There is no parent that is willing to allow a child to have its *own way in everything—i. e.*, if a wise parent. When at the General Conference of 1848 the committee reported a separate conference for the colored members within the Church "inexpedient," what was thought of it? Was it, under the then existing circumstances, impracticable and inexpedient? It was most assuredly impracticable, in that but few localities would allow slaves to have a meeting of their own in the absence of some white person. The Lord Jesus said: "I came not to destroy the law, but to fulfill the law." He verified this by paying taxes, and observing (and having others do the same) the Jewish law. Suppose the Church, at that time, had given them a separate conference for Maryland and Delaware, could they have enjoyed the benefits of it? Most assuredly not. On the other hand, it would have undoubtedly weakened the influence of the Church with the masters, and subjected the colored members to restrictions of privileges, and brought upon them uncalled-for hardships.

The tasks imposed upon the poor Hebrews in Egypt were increased, as well as the inflictions of punishment, as soon as they began to believe in Moses' plan of a "three days' journey into the wilderness to worship God." When a desire for a separate conference came from those who could enjoy it without let, it was at once arranged for them. I believe the more intelligent colored men listened to the words of advice and wisdom of the General Conference with confidence. And yet it must be declared that many of the influential colored members of our Church were urged up to the belief that it was refused them from mere jealousy on the part of 'the white folks,' because they did not want the colored man elevated; because they wished to boss him in Church matters as his master did in every-day affairs.

Very many advantages were offered the African Churches by the failure of our Church to grant the requests made by our members for separate annual conferences. Whether they took advantage of them or not, a great many people in these United States believe they did. Every time the General Conference was asked to grant separate conferences, and it did not do so because of its impracticability, it was not strange that they were vexed, hearing everywhere, "I told you *colored folks* so." As a result of such failure we lost, from 1844 until we were granted separate conferences, not less than one-fourth of the membership of the African Churches in this country at that time. As strange as it may seem, it is really true. But probably the Church was not to be blamed altogether for not doing for the colored members that which would have inevitably worked hardships for them in the slaveholding States. But why did not the Church at once form separate conferences for our people in those States where the African and African Zion Churches were then operating? As we turn these questions over in our minds, several valid reasons occur to us. Either because the Church loved the colored man, and wanted him to have his own choice when allowed to enjoy it—whether for separate congregations, conferences, or Churches—even though they all declared a desire to unite with one of the two colored organizations, or both of them, already in existence, and thus become a religious power in those States where it was practicable, in the which they could still aid them; or because the Church thought the world would declare—had they organized another colored Church—that they were following with opposition and spite those two bodies, by setting up a "colored Church" within a white one to break those two down; or the Church did not want to move in the matter until somewhat of the outcome of the Negro question could be seen or known; or else, because they really thought it the duty of the Methodist Episcopal Church to look after those colored members in the slave States where "the colored organizations" could not go, and abandon all other colored members as material for the upbuilding of their work. The latter, I believe, is nearer the truth. And by this is not meant that they refused to allow colored members to join the Church, or to commune with it in the "free States," but that *no special pains were put forth to induce them to join the Methodist Episcopal Church where either of those bodies had charge.* This is one of the advantages they have enjoyed over the colored members remaining in the Methodist Episcopal Church. Again, may it not be surmised that since ours is "the Prince of peace," and rivalry in ecclesiastical, as other matters, usually is followed by strife, that the refusal of the Church to grant separate conferences to the colored members in those States was but an effort to avoid strife?   Again, for the Church to have granted separate conferences, as a stay against the secession spirit manifested in 1816 and 1823, would have been considered by a great many good people—and used to advantage by the seceders—as a declaration of the charges made by the African Churches that "the whites were anxious to get rid of the colored element within the Church."   From whatever point we take cognizance of that matter, it would appear as if the Church tried to do what was for the best. Every conceivable thing was done to pacify and keep the colored members within the Church. The secession of the Wesleyans had a great deal to do with the complication of this matter, for they were, in many instances, naturally the main stay for African Methodism.

THE FIRST COLORED BISHOP IN THE METHODIST EPISCOPAL CHURCH.

The interest the Methodist Episcopal Church had in the colored man was not confined to America.

> "The old Church sought her sheep,
>   The parent sought her child;
> She followed him o'er vale and hill,
>   O'er deserts waste and wild;
> She found him nigh to death,
>   Famished, and faint, and lone;
> She bound him with the bands of love,
>   She saved the wandering one."

The first foreign mission-field of the Methodist Episcopal Church was Africa. When the "freed people" of these United States began to move to the west coast of that country, the Church began to follow them by sending over missionaries to-look after her colored members and others who would accept the service. From time to time the membership multiplied, and in 1833 a mission was organized and then an annual conference. This missionary field may have been the outgrowth of the seeds sown by Dr. Coke, who in 1814, on his voyage to India, left a missionary at the Cape of Good Hope. The work continued to increase until it was declared by some the leaven that was to leaven Africa. In 1834, in company with Rev. John Seys, was sent Rev. Francis Burns from New York, he having been ordained deacon and elder by that man of God, Bishop Janes. In 1849 he was appointed presiding elder of the Cape Palmas District of the Liberia Annual Conference. When the General Conference of 1856 convened in the city of Indianapolis, Indiana, a new phase of the colored membership question came up. Africa was knocking at the door of the conference, asking for a missionary bishop. The General Conference at once took up the cry, examined the matter, and requested the Liberia Annual Conference to select the man. This was done by the selecting of Rev. Francis Burns. He at once prepared to return to America for ordination.

Why did the Methodist Episcopal Church not send a bishop by the West Coast of Africa and have him ordained there? Why bring him back to America, where the colored man was only recognized as a chattel, a bondman, a serf? And yet, to her praise be it said, she did for the colored man in America what *no other denomination* found it convenient to do—ordained a colored man to the episcopacy. When Rev. Francis Burns arrived he was given all the honor any man could have expected. He was accordingly ordained at the session of the Genesee Conference, October 14, 1858, the services being conducted by Bishops Janes and Baker. But after all this, what did the Church really think and say concerning this colored man at that time? The assembly that witnessed his ordination, and those who grasped his ebony hand and bid him God-speed, declare in the words of Dr. Robie, who was present: "Though of ebony complexion, he had gained wonderfully on the affection and respect of all who had made his acquaintance, and especially those privileged to an intimate association with him. His manner is exceedingly pleasant, and his spirit kind, sweet, and good as ever beamed from human heart or disposition. He seems to be lacking in none of the qualifications of the gentleman and Christian minister. He possesses also an intelligent and cultivated mind, speaks readily and fluently, and even eloquently, and is in all respects a model African. Such is the man whom the Liberia Conference has selected for a bishop, and such the one the highest authorities of our American Church have set apart for the sacred and responsible position." We add, Thus shall it be done to *the colored man* whom the Methodist Episcopal Church delights to honor on slave soil, where prejudice against the race grew as rank as wild weeds.

The election and ordination of Bishop Burns was not a subterfuge, for the Church elected another colored man to the episcopacy—Rev. John W. Roberts, in 1866—one year after the war closed. He was consecrated in St. Paul's Methodist Episcopal Church, in New York City, June 20th of that year.

With the interests of the race at heart, what more could she have done?

But the advance steps already taken by the Church on that question were twisted by those who opposed the Church in her efforts to do God's will toward the downtrodden race, into every shape but the proper one. The cry still went up from at least two sources that the Church was not willing to recognize the colored ministry and members within her borders. The colored members within the Church where such attacks were made still felt that a further step *must* be taken by the Church to save the colored membership. So there came up to that General Conference from the colored members within the Baltimore, Philadelphia, and New Jersey

Conferences one or more memorials, all of which were referred to a special committee, which reported as follows:

"The committee to whom were referred the memorials of colored members within the bounds of the Baltimore, Philadelphia, and New Jersey Conferences, after due consideration, report the following for the adoption of the conference, and recommend that it be inserted in the Discipline as a distinct chapter, entitled,

"CHAPTER VIII. OF THE RIGHTS AND PRIVI-
LEGES OF OUR COLORED MEMBERS.

" 1. Our colored preachers and official members shall have all the privileges which are usual to others in quarterly conferences, where the usages of the country do not forbid it. And the presiding elder may hold for them a separate quarterly conference when in his judgment it shall be expedient.

" 2. The bishop or presiding elder may employ colored preachers to travel and preach, when their services are judged necessary: *Provided*, that no one shall be so employed without having been recommended by a quarterly conference.

" 3. The bishops may call a conference once in each year of our colored local preachers, within the bounds of any one or more of our districts, for the purpose of conferring with them with respect to the wants of the work among our colored people, and the best means to be employed in promoting its prosperity; at which conference the presiding elder within whose district, and under whose care the colored charges and congregations are, shall be present: *Provided,* that the holding of said conference or conferences shall be recommended by an annual conference, and the bishops, upon due inquiry, shall deem it practicable and expedient."

Again, by this action, the Church recognized the colored members within her communion as being *eligible to all privileges* usual to other members, showing at once that her heart was all right.

THE FIRST EDUCATIONAL EFFORT.

By this is not meant that no interest in the education of the race had been manifested prior to this. The education of Bishop Burns, alone, would refute such an idea. But the Church began to see and feel that something on a larger scale ought to be done for the higher education of the colored youth within the Church. The very idea points out the fact that the Church saw for her colored members a better day coming. At the General Conference above mentioned, *Wilberforce University,* now in the hands of our brethren of the African Church, at Xenia, Ohio, was purchased by a number of individuals, and was under the patronage of the Cincinnati Conference of our Church, and was "devoted to the higher education of colored youth." Rev. J. F. Wright, D. D., its efficient agent, presented its claims to the General Conference. He traveled in its interest, and it continued to flourish.

Rev. R. S. Rust, D D., became president of this institution in 1859. Our brethren of the African Church began to feel the need of a better educated ministry, and having no outlook for such an institution turned their attention toward this institution. Bishop D. A. Payne, having formed the acquaintance of President Rust, began negotiations for the transfer of that property to the African Methodist Episcopal Church; and, in 1863, it accordingly "passed into their hands for *a nominal sum.*" Thus the beginning of the educational work in the African Methodist Episcopal Church was but the outgrowth of the generosity of the Methodist Episcopal Church toward the colored race, whether within or without the Church. It is true that but little, if any, credit is ever given to the Church that was represented in the matter by our own Dr. R. S. Rust. They sometimes—and Bishop Payne all the time—mention gratefully his name, but no public acknowledgment by that Church has yet been made to us for the advantages given them in this transaction; and hence many a student, who has attended there, has gone away ignorant of these facts. That transaction is but another proof of the fact that but little, if any, opposition or rivalry has ever been allowed from our Church toward their Church.

It did seem that, ecclesiastically as well as politically, "Providence had wisely mingled their cup." When one phase of the question touching slavery

NEW ORLEANS UNIVERSITY—MAIN BUILDING.

had been met, another phase developed. If ecclesiasticism met this "sum of all villainies" in its way, and struck it down, leaving it wounded, bleeding, and dying, it would, phœnix-like, the next day appear in the political field. Like "Banquo's ghost," it would not down at the bidding. The General Conference of 1856 had hardly adjourned before the political world was startled by the case of a colored man—Dred Scott—which was brought before the courts for decision. The appeal was brought up to the Supreme Court. Chief Justice Tancy, speaking for the court, declared in this case that "Negroes, whether free or slaves, are not citizens of the United States, and they can not become such by any process known to the Constitution." This decision caused a ripple, not only on the sea of politics, but over the placid stream of Methodism; for it must not appear or be considered egotism when it is said nothing relating to the interests of the colored man has transpired in this country in which Methodism did not take part. And yet, as strange as it may appear, the Church has always objected to mixing politics with religion; but believing the converse admissible, our Church papers began to wage war in favor of this colored man, as if he had been a member of the Methodist Episcopal Church.

This excitement had not subsided when Abraham Lincoln, as the nominee of the Republican party, was elected President of the United States.

The relation our Church sustained to that conflict will be better understood when it is remembered that Torrey and Lovejoy, the two martyrs to the Abolition cause, were New England ministers; that the New England Methodists very early identified themselves with this cause, and poured hot shot into the foul slave oligarchy. As early as June 4, 1835, the New England Conference of the Methodist Episcopal Church had organized an anti-slavery society—not simply a non-partisan, namby-pamby sort of a stay-at-home-and-pray society, but active, vigilant, and progressive—on the basis of the immediate and unconditional abolition of slavery. North Bennett Street Methodist Episcopal Church, in Boston, was opened in that year for Rev. George Thompson to preach a sermon against slavery. William Lloyd Garrison spoke of that meeting as follows:

"In these days of slavish servility and malignant prejudices, we are presented occasionally with some beautiful specimens of Christian obedience and courage. One of these is seen in the opening of the North Bennett Street Methodist Episcopal meeting-house in Boston to the advocates for the honor of God, the salvation of our country, and the freedom of enslaved millions in our midst. As the pen of the historian, in after years, shall trace the rise, progress, and glorious triumph of the Abolition cause, he will delight to record, and posterity will delight to read, that when all other pulpits were dumb, all other churches closed on the subject of slavery in Boston, the boasted 'cradle of liberty,' there was one pulpit that would speak out, one Church that would throw open its doors in behalf of the downtrodden victims of American tyranny, and that was the pulpit and Church above alluded to. The primitive spirit of Methodism is beginning to revive with all its holy zeal and courage, and it will not falter until all the Methodist Churches are purged from the pollution of slavery, and the last slave in the land stands forth a redeemed and regenerated being."

Notwithstanding the above, such Methodist ministers as Rev. Gilbert Haven and others kept the ball rolling. It is said of one of our bishops: "Throughout the late contest Bishop Simpson did much to strengthen the hands of President Lincoln, and to nerve the spirit of the nation to endure any sacrifice for the cause of the Union." Is it any wonder, then, that the Church, in one way or the other, was connected with nearly every effort for the emancipation of the slaves? Therefore the eighteenth session of the General Conference that convened in the city of Buffalo, May, 1860, was anticipated with much anxiety.

The great debate on the question of slavery at the last General Conference had, during this entire quadrennium, proven sufficient to keep up the agitation all along the line. Dr. Abel Stevens, then editor of the *Christian Advocate*, addressed an

"Appeal" to the general Church "concerning what the next General Conference should do on the question of slavery." This appeal aimed simply to have the next General Conference declare "the sense of the Church on the whole subject," with "a note, put in the margin of the General Rule," that declared "the only cases of slaveholding admissible to our communion are such as are consistent with the Golden Rule." Drs. Nathan Bangs and J. H. Perry, at the head of a "Ministers' and Laymen's Union," formed within the New York Conference in 1859, and the Anti-slavery Society, with Dr. Curry leading, hurled their anathemas against Dr. Stevens's proposition. Resolutions favoring a new rule on slavery, prior to the General Conference of 1860, were voted upon as follows: Cincinnati, 319 votes for, 1,212 votes against it; Providence, 1,242 for, and 1,329 votes against it; Erie, 1,795 for, and 1,416 votes against it. It was conceded that the cause of human liberty would receive a fresh impetus from the ringing speeches that would be delivered, and from the solid resolutions that would be passed at that General Conference. Accordingly two classes of petitions were presented: "Those asking for the extirpation of slavery from the Church," and "those asking that no change be made in the Discipline on the subject of slavery." A special committee was ordered to receive resolutions of this kind. There was also appointed "a Committee on our Colored Membership." Several

memorials and petitions from our colored membership were presented. After due consideration, notwithstanding the excitement on account of the
agitation of the question of slavery, that committee
reported as follows:

"The Committee on Colored Membership, to
which were referred certain memorials from colored
local preachers, respectfully represent: That having examined said memorials, they find that they
request this body, (1) To extend the bounds of the
conference of colored local preachers, called in ac-
cordance with the provisions introduced into the Discipline at the last General Conference; (2) To grant
them the power to try and expel their own members;
(3) To confer upon the conference of colored local
preachers power to elect to deacons' and elders' orders; (4) To invest said conference with all the powers
of a regular annual conference; (5) To admit colored preachers to membership in our annual conferences. Your committee find that the first two objects
prayed for are, in substance, covered by provisions
already existing in the Discipline, which appear to
have been overlooked by the petitioners. In regard to items three and four, referred to above,
your committee find that the prayer of the memorialists could not be granted without doing violence
to our usages and Disciplinary regulations. The
fifth item embraced in the memorials before us was
withdrawn by the representative of the petitioners,
who appeared in person before the committee. In

view of the whole of the foregoing, your committee recommend that the whole subject be dismissed. All of which is respectfully submitted.

"S. Y. Monroe, Chairman."

When the Committee on Slavery reported, there were submitted a "majority" and a "minority" report, a substitute for the majority report. The first resolution of the committee was:

"*Resolved*, by the delegates of the several annual conferences, in General Conference assembled, That we recommend the amendment of the General Rule on Slavery, so that it shall read: 'The buying, selling, or holding of men, women, or children, with an intention to enslave them.'"

This motion was lost, since it required a two-thirds vote; and 138 voted for it, and 74 against it. The second resolution was:

"*Resolved*, That we recommend the suspension of the fourth Restrictive Rule, for the purpose set forth in the foregoing resolution."

The first resolution having failed, this was laid on the table. The third was:

"*Resolved*, by the delegates of the several annual conferences, in General Conference assembled, That the following be, and hereby is, substituted in the place of the seventh chapter on Slavery: *Question.* What shall be done for the extirpation of slavery? *Answer.* We declare that we are as much as ever convinced of the great evil of slavery. We believe that the buying, selling, or holding of human beings as chattels, is contrary to the laws of God and nature, inconsistent with the Golden Rule, and with that rule in our Discipline which requires all who desire to remain among us to 'do no harm, and to avoid evil of every kind.' We therefore affectionately admonish all our preachers and people to keep themselves pure from this great evil, and to seek its extirpation by all lawful and Christian means."

This was necessarily the last work of the General Conference of the Methodist Episcopal Church on behalf of the colored man before the terrible Civil War in this country, that began during the ensuing quadrennium.

CHAPTER V.

THE RETROSPECT.

WHO has not, ere this, declared slavery a vice? We have seen that the Methodist Episcopal Church in 1796 not only warned its members against the vice of holding their fellow-men, their brethren, as slaves, but required a guarantee from applicants for membership that, if owners of slaves, they would manumit them at the earliest possible moment; if not, that they would not engage in it while in the communion of the Church; that if "any among us do not wish to abide by this rule, they shall have the privilege quietly to withdraw." Such a spirit was in keeping with the Ten Commandments and the Sermon on the Mount. Not only this, but any member of the Methodist Episcopal Church who should sell a human being for any reason, was to be expelled. In cases where members of the Church bought colored people, even though done for the purpose of keeping husband and wife together, or from being separated, it was stipulated that such should only be held in servitude a sufficient time to pay back to the purchaser the price paid for him or her. This plan, in itself, was not only a wise business transaction for the liberation of slaves, but humane and just; creditable to the Church and honorable in the purchaser when done willingly, as well as elevating in its very nature, and calculated to put the slave under perpetual gratitude to his liberator. The plan was unique, and if it had been observed in every such case throughout the length and breadth of this fair land, our American civilization would have become the ideal of the world. If our government had but consented to adopt some such measure looking to the gradual liberation of the slaves, is it not rational to believe the late Civil War could have been averted, and many precious lives and much property been saved? But the American people apparently did not view it in that light. It came at last, as of old, the arbitrary Pharaoh rushed on pursuing his slaves, notwithstanding the terrible warnings given, until ingulfed in the boisterous waves of the mighty Red Sea. How true is it that "the wicked pass on, and are punished!" No more fearful punishment ever came upon any nation than came upon ours because of slavery. Although the above plan was adopted by the Church, it declared that if a Methodist person purchased a slave woman, all her children—whether her husband was a free man or not—were to be free from birth. Thus the Church sought at once to begin emancipation.

The General Conference of 1800 declared slavery among ministers or lay members not only " reprehensible," but that "such slaveholders must consent to manumit all such persons held in bondage

or leave the Church," even though purchased
to prevent the separation of husband and wife, or
parents and children. Thus the Church unmistakably declared its unutterable opposition to the
heretical doctrine of "doing evil that good may
come of it." That General Conference, if possible,
went further still when it declared: "Any minister
who marries a slaveholding wife must be expelled."
If this was not strong language, then there is
none. The Church, at that period, sought not only
to protect, but to give "the colored members
within its communion all the rights and privileges
guaranteed by the Discipline to any other members." Was it strange, after this action, that the
Methodist Episcopal Church decided that even colored men were eligible to ordination? From henceforth the Church saw no valid reason, as there
was none, why it should not be done; and hence
the Church began to ordain colored men as "deacons in the Church of God."

We have seen that at each General Conference of our Church from the beginning, the question of human slavery was discussed, opposed, and
anathematized by the Church. And yet during
that time many strange things occurred. In the General Conference of 1804, that met in the city of
Baltimore, Freeborn Garrettson moved that the
question of the buying and selling of slaves be left
to the three bishops for regulation. Just what this
meant does not appear on the surface. It could

have meant that the Church knew the hearts of the three bishops were right, and that they would therefore oppose anything like a compromise with the system of human slavery then in vogue. It could have meant that they were conservative, and would not, therefore, likely precipitate any trouble upon the Church on account of this vexed question. Viewed from any point at this distance, it assumes a strange attitude. It may have been intended as a measure to "bring peace out of confusion;" but "peace," "peace," when there could be no peace, had been the slaveholders' cry all along. It was considered a conciliatory measure. It proved to be exactly the reverse. It resulted in confusion; for the following General Conference, in 1808, declared that the question of "buying and selling slaves must hereafter be left to the discretion of the several annual conferences for decision. Though this action was taken seventy-nine years ago, it appears as inexplicable to the writer as it did to some men at that day. Its consistency and spirit do not even to-day present a single redeeming feature. Every General Conference had moved a notch higher in opposition to slavery, and now the whole subject was ordered out of the General Conference, to be decided by the annual conferences, in the which were some probably, if not slaveholders, sympathizers with slavery. This was done, too, in face of the well-known fact that the United States government had become so disturbed on account of the discussions arising out of the question of human slavery and other causes, as to prohibit the importation of any more African slaves into America. It could have been one of those peculiar proceedings that occur now and then, in the which "certain inalienable rights, among which life, liberty, and the pursuit of happiness" have no consideration; but in the which "expediency," and not principle, obtain. It is thought by some that the action taken by that General Conference on the question of slavery was regretted by many afterward. The motion by which that question was sent down to the annual conferences was a repetition of the political idea of the doctrine of States' rights, with the colored man's interests not considered.

When the General Conference met in the city of Baltimore in 1812, the persistency of the friends of the colored man in pushing his claims showed him not friendless. The colored man, like other men, feels very keenly impositions, and yet we think it is conceded that he is of a religious turn of mind, docile and humble, but has his preferences as clearly as other men. He does not like to be considered a bone of contention, a cat's-paw, or an intruder. He does like to have his manhood respected. But suppose the above action of the General Conference of 1808 was a mistake, is it not admissible that it was possible to turn the head of the Church in the opposite direction now and then, if even for a time only? It was a perplexing question, indeed; and as the law of the land supported it—for slavery shielded itself behind the venerated Constitution—what more could the Church do, since some conferences were in Massachusetts and some in South Carolina? However, that General Conference declared that under existing circumstances but little, if anything, could be done to abolish human slavery in America outside of political powers; that the Church of God in general, and the Methodist Episcopal Church in particular, could not reach the question as effectively as the civil law. But the civil law had only then begun to take notice of the foul system of slavery in this country.

In the despondency of that day and hour—for there was despondency behind the action of that body on the question of slavery—the attention of that General Conference was called to consider the advisability of looking after the interests of "the free people of color." In some States the manumission of slaves was prohibited, except they were at once moved out of that State. In cases where this was not done some complaint would usually be lodged against them, and they were incarcerated in prison, and, "as a penalty for violation of the law, were sold again into slavery by sheriff's sale." Colonization in Africa was seemingly the only hope. Hence, when a report was presented to the General Conference from the American Colonization Society, it was commended to the generous public. Such cases as that of Dred Scott discouraged many people who wished to manumit their slaves from doing so, for fear they might be re-enslaved. The General Conference declared the idea of colonizing the "free people of color" in Africa as a wise measure in the right direction. What less could the Church have done for the race? What less ought it to have done? When the General Conference of 1816 met, the question of slavery, and the proper recognition of the colored members of the Church came up for consideration. The Church must have seen by that time that a mistake had been made by refusing to grant its colored members a separate conference. Not that the Church had given colored members of intelligence "cause for complaint," but that it did not sooner see that an insidious foe was in its very vitals, stealing away its life. If the Church, however, had been an institution dependent upon the whims of the human family, whose strength and perpetuation were dependent wholly upon its agreement with the slave oligarchy, the action taken by the Church in defense of her colored members would have appeared fool-hardy. But it was not, for it had the support of Him who said, "Upon this rock I will build my Church, and the gates of hell shall not prevail against it."

The secession of the "Allenites" alienated quite a number of Christian men from the side of the defense of the colored man. Why should it not, when a few of the faithful white men had not only jeoparded their future prospects, blighted their present fame, brought down upon them the vituperation and obloquy of the slave oligarchy within and without the Church, simply because they professed to believe "a man's a man for a' that, and a' that?" Is it not strange that some were so unwise as to be misled by a misguiding or ambitious spirit, when they were not able to add one cubit to their stature or make one hair white or black?

During the ensuing quadrennium "the color question" was discussed pro and con. When the General Conference of 1824 met in Baltimore, and declared that colored preachers were entitled to equal privileges "with others," it was a commendable step. Such action was calculated to restore to the fold the seceders of 1816 and 1820, had their ambition not reached beyond justice and right. Although the Methodist Episcopal Church did all in its power, apparently, by General Conference action and episcopal supervision, to reclaim the seceders, they persistently refused either to be comforted or to return to the fold. Probably sufficient cause can be found in Bishop Allen's reasons for not wishing to accept Bishop Asbury's invitation to travel and preach with him, when the reason as given by him to the bishop was, that he thought "that men should lay up something for a rainy day." There was never a promise made by the Master to give any man a large salary to hunt up "the lost sheep of Israel." Because of the failure to conciliate those offended brethren some looked askant at Methodism; because, forsooth, they knew not the bottom facts. From the General Conference of 1824 to that of 1836, which met in Cincinnati, Ohio, the agitation of the question continued. The condemnation of the two premature lecturers by this General Conference gave great offense to the Abolitionists everywhere, and depressed woefully the spirits of the colored members without the Church. Poor, ignorant, and deluded men would naturally and rightfully conclude that in the hearts and bosoms of those men their dearest interests were planted, and hence the disposition to put a quietus upon them was equivalent to the non-recognition of the rights of the colored man within and without the Church to the bright anticipation of ever being allowed the enjoyment of " life, liberty, and the pursuit of happiness." As a natural result of the supposed compromise with slavery made by the "Conference Rights" act, many conferences complained by memorial that they had difficulty after difficulty in properly adjusting the matter of slavery. Hence came the next step—legitimate child of previous action—a declaration that the question of slavery was one of those peculiar cases where only the civil law could properly adjust and act upon it. From 1836 to 1844 the war on slavery and in favor of slavery was unceasingly waged within and without the Church. The thought of the regular succession of events is not to be questioned when we remember the struggles of the General Conference of 1840 at Baltimore over the appeal of Silas Comfort, and that of the marriage of a Baltimorean preacher and a Georgian bishop to slaveholding women. The Silas Comfort decision was, on the whole, the best thing possible for the peace of the colored man within and without the Methodist Episcopal Church. The decision was all that could have been asked so far as the then present peace of the colored man was concerned. But the Lord Jesus at one time said: "I came not to bring peace on the earth, but a sword." If we have the proper conception of his meaning, there are times when peace is not the best thing possible. When the General Conference received the protest from Sharp Street Church against the decision, it only exhibited the fact that men and Churches do not always see themselves as others see them.

But if in the Silas Comfort appeal decision the enemies of human rights scored a victory over the friends of human freedom, the latter turned the tide and scored a more glorious as well as righteous victory at the General Conference of 1844, that met in the city of New York, when the resolution that had been carried and placed on record denouncing the action of "the two Abolition lecturers" was ordered to be expunged therefrom. At that General Conference a petition was presented from the colored ministers within the Church asking admission into the annual

conferences. This was refused for some reason.
Then there followed a petition for a separate conference. The wisdom of the refusal to grant said
separate conference is now apparent to all who are
either concerned or have the interests of the race,
as such, at heart. No argument is needed to sub-
stantiate the above proposition in the minds of any
intelligent person. Notwithstanding this, the historian of African Methodism said in his " Apology:"
" It would have been a source of unspeakable joy
had he been permitted truthfully to record that
your Church had acknowledged your full and true
manhood, and not denied it both in practice and in
law—had received you into conference upon a perfect ministerial equality; but, alas! the doors of its
conferences were locked, and bolted and barred
against you." Such thrusts as the above, if there
was no other sufficient reason for asking it, were
certainly calculated to urge the matter forward,
because. the restlessness of the members, begotten
by such unsolicited and sophisticated sympathy,
showed it necessary. Just why separate conferences
were not given them in the free States does not
appear on the surface. Those who were in authority
at that time no doubt had good and sufficient
reasons for not granting the privilege of membership with white ministers in the annual conferences
on the one hand, nor separate conferences on the
other hand. While it does not appear that it would
have been wisdom to have granted them the latter

in the slave States, we submit, now, without questioning the wisdom displayed by those godly fathers. Those who wish to speculate may do so; we are satisfied.   All this but declares

> "Vice is a monster of so frightful mien,
> As to be hated, needs but to be seen;
> Yet seen too oft, familiar with her face,
> We first endure, then pity, then embrace."

CHAPTER VI.

DURING THE WAR.

THE Abolition Church! If there was any one denomination of Christians in this country, north of Mason and Dixon's Line, that was anathematized beyond another, declared by many in the South one of the most forward instigators and abettors of the late Civil War, it was the "Northern" or "Abolition Methodist Church," as they called our Church. Well do I remember the "yarns" told by the soldiers of General Sterling Price's army on a preacher they captured from the Union soldiers in Missouri. The preacher was a noble specimen, and looked more like a Norman king than any of those about him. This minister of the Lord Jesus was terribly abused by his captors. Not so much, as they said, because he was a Union soldier—that was bad enough—but he belonged to the "Northern" or "Abolition Methodist Church." "The Methodist Episcopal Church, South"—or as it is, and was, better known as "The Southern Methodist Episcopal Church"—is a relative term or name. It was natural, therefore, for the Southern Confederacy to adopt it, and grant it a kind of supremacy above every other denomination. Did it not lead the secession movement in favor of slavery? It is no stretch of imagination to say some people united

with it for that very reason. It was to have been
expected that the two Churches, wherever they met,
would sustain the same relations that the Jews and
Samaritans used to sustain to each other. It was
impossible to expect anything less than bitter opposition to the "Northern Church." There was a
time in the South when he who spoke favorably
of our Church was not only suspected as a "lover
of niggers," but one to be "let alone," for all
intents and purposes, as a traitor. That times have
changed but very little in the South along these
lines, but few doubt.

If there never comes another time and cause
when the Methodist Episcopal Church will interest
herself in the politics of this country, no sane
person will deny the fact that she was so interested
when the question of the abolition of human slavery
was being discussed, and while the Civil War was
being waged. If there has never been a time when
"the two branches of Methodism" hung on exactly
opposite sides of the parent tree with about equal
weight since the secession of 1844 until the Civil
War began, they occupied the above-named attitude
during the bloody scenes of those four years. The
Methodist Episcopal Church, South, as such, supported the Confederacy, while the Methodist Episcopal Church supported the Union. And now if
the Methodist Episcopal Church, South, closed her
doors that the pastor might lead his official lay
members into the war—praying, preaching, singing,

and fighting every day of the week and Sunday,
too—the Methodist Episcopal Church did as much
to counteract this. The evidence of this is found
in the fact that for upwards of twenty years—ever
since the secession of 1844 to 1864—the Methodist
Episcopal Church had been practically excluded
from the South, and only ventured to plant outposts
along the border States, where she found admittance
by some compromises to the conservative element
that came to her there. Not only so, but President
Lincoln declared it "no fault of other denominations that the Methodist Episcopal Church fur-
nished more money and men to suppress the Rebellion." As a rule our bishops and ministers and
membership, wherever they went, preached, lectured,
exhorted, and prayed for the overthrow of the terrible slavery that bound hand and foot four and
a half million human beings in a bondage more
terrible than that of Pharaoh and more demoralizing
than that of the Russian empire. It was said of one
of our bishops: "Throughout the late war Bishop
Simpson did much to strengthen the hands of President Lincoln, and to nerve the spirit of the nation
to endure any sacrifice for the cause of the Union."

The class of men elected to General Conference
positions at the General Conference of 1860, showed
unmistakably the attitude of our Church toward
slavery and the war. Her standing rule that " non-
slaveholding" henceforth was to be one of the conditions of membership in the Church, the periodi-

cals of the Church being put in the hands of
anti-slavery editors were straws in the wind.
Everybody knows that Dr. Daniel Wise was considered "an offensive partisan" on the question of
slavery. Dr. Whedon, who was barely elected at
the General Conference of 1856 because of his
radicalism, was at this General Conference (1860)
unanimously re-elected editor of our *Quarterly Review*. When that General Conference adjourned it
was plainly to be seen that our Church had put on
ecclesiastical war-paint, and was therefore prepared
to push the battle of human freedom to the gate.
If any one doubts this, proof is forthcoming in the
fact that, the conservative element in our Church
seeing the status of affairs, a newspaper, known as
The Methodist, was established by them in New
York City. The following March, when the Baltimore Annual Conference met, it resolved, by a unanimous vote, that it was "determined not to hold connection with any ecclesiastical body that makes
non-slaveholding a condition of membership in the
Church." Indeed, so high did opposition to the
position the Church had taken on slavery rise, that
another secession, similar to that of 1844, came
near taking place. When Rev. Mr. Hedrick was
presented by the Baltimore Conference for ordination to Bishop Scott, he publicly excepted the new
chapter on slavery. Bishop Scott then arose and said:
" I regard myself restrained from ordaining any one
who declines to take upon him the ordination vows

without qualification or exception. Hence, I can not ordain Mr. Hedrick." This caused considerable commotion, but the bishop stood like the rock of Gibraltar. "There were giants in those days" all about him, whose reputation for wisdom and influence was enviable. The lay conference was in session at the same time in the city. When they were informed of the refusal of Bishop Scott to ordain Mr. Hedrick, and the reasons given, they took action declaring a disposition to ignore the entire subject of slavery in the Discipline. When it is remembered what class of people our Methodism claims in the State of Maryland; their means, influence, and their disposition to lead matters, since it (Baltimore) may be considered one of the principal cradles of Methodism, and has all along been in the van of Methodist movements; that some of the most influential, eloquent, and popular men in the Methodist Episcopal Church "were born in her," it adds intensity and alarm to the situation. But Bishop Scott, like most of our bishops, knew the heart of the Church; knew that he was in full accord with the Church on the question of slavery, and therefore the Lord was on his side, and stood like Martin Luther before the Diet at Worms, trusting in God. When such an expression of opinion on the question of slavery was given by "the sinews of war"—the laymen—it was an inspiration to the clerical brethren of the Baltimore Annual Conference. The soul of Bishop Scott was severely taxed, the Methodist Episcopal Church was disturbed, while the very air seemed laden with dust from the recent conflict, and more especially when the Baltimore Annual Conference responded to the expression of opinion given by the lay conference, by declaring in open conference: "If three-fourths of all the annual conferences will, within the year 1861, agree with us, we agree with the action of the laymen and the Baltimore Conference, and will not reunite with them in Church fellowship." When this was presented to the conference, Bishop Scott announced that he could not entertain a motion contemplating a division of the Church. He permitted the secretary, Rev. J. S. Martin, to put the question. But when the bishop came to the chair he ordered the following paper spread upon the journal:

"The whole action just had on what is called the 'Norval Wilson propositions' is, in my judgment, in violation of the order and Discipline of the Methodist Episcopal Church, and therefore is null and void, regarded as conference action. I, therefore, do not recognize such action as infracting the integrity of this body, and so I shall proceed to finish the business of the present session.

"Levi Scott."

The East Baltimore Conference was also on the eve of seceding, while the Philadelphia Conference signified its willingness, by a vote of 174 to 35, to have the Rule on Slavery changed. These facts were enough in themselves to cause the South to look askant at the Methodist Episcopal Church, and probably caused the Church to be nicknamed "the Abolition Church."

By this time the rumors of war had reached a climax. We find a proper description in the language of the historian Ridpath, who, in speaking of the capture of Fort Sumter by the rebels, says:

"The news of this startling event went through the country like a flame of fire. There had been some expectation of violence, but the actual shock came like a clap of thunder. The people of the towns poured into the streets, and the country folk flocked to the villages to gather the tidings and to comment on the coming conflict. Gray-haired men talked gravely of the deed that was done, and prophesied of its consequences. Public opinion, both in the North and the South, was rapidly consolidated. Three days after the fall of Fort Sumter, President Lincoln issued a call for seventy-five thousand volunteers to serve three months in the overthrow of the secession movement. On the 19th of April, when the first regiments of Massachusetts volunteers were passing through Baltimore on their way to Washington, they were fired upon by the citizens and three men killed."

The sounds of preparation for war were heard in every direction. No less spirit was being manifested throughout the Methodist Episcopal Church. And yet, notwithstanding the fact that the Baltimore Annual Conference withdrew by resolution from the Methodist Episcopal Church, because the Church stood up for the poor slave, not a single compromise at that time was made by the Church with slavery. To get some idea of the condition of affairs at the time, or directly thereafter, when Bishop Levi Scott stood up in the face of the whole world and let his light so shine that men might see his good works and those of the Church he represented, when he declined to ordain the Rev. Mr. Hedrick in the presence of the Baltimore Conference, we quote the language of a man whom every colored man and most good white men love to honor—Gilbert Haven, D. D.—who says in his description of the "First War Sunday:"

"That Sabbath-day's journey ought to be chronicled. We marched through saintly Boston in the gray twilight to the tune of 'Yankee Doodle.' All along the route cannons and bells, bands and flags and waving handkerchiefs, soldiers and crowds upon crowds, gave us a hearty hail and farewell. At Hartford we were told the women were all at home driving their sewing-machines, and the men busy making cartridges for their troops. All the town left their churches and gathered around the depot, where they had had preaching and singing while waiting for us. They had also provided refreshments enough for five thousand persons, and plied us with sweetmeats and benedictions. The force of the fever could go no farther."

The colored man from one end of this country to the other had always recognized the Methodist Episcopal Church as a friend to him and his, a friend whose sympathies were worth a great deal. But whenever he was reminded that it was "The Abolition Church" and one of the prime causes of the war—which was usually taught him whenever the poor, deluded colored men imagined, as they would naturally at times, that the war imposed additional hardships and burdens—he sometimes shuddered. But when the Union forces went South, and any of the colored people were seen, they usually spoke kindly to them. If about religious matters, they usually found the colored man either a Baptist or a Methodist. If the latter, and the interlocutor, or any one of the company, was a Methodist, the poor colored man learned of the interest the Church was taking in his welfare and liberation. When colored men ran within the Federal lines, they never failed to find the chaplain or some one of the company a member of the Methodist Church, who deeply sympathized with him, and did all possible to make him comfortable. While all this was true, another aspect presented itself.

THE ATTITUDE OF THE CHURCH AS SEEN BY GENERAL CONFERENCE ACTION.

It was not enough that the General Conference had repeatedly stood forth the friend of the Union, but individual conferences gave no uncertain sound at that time. It is almost literally true that the hitherto unmistakable factional lines within the Church faded so much that the anti-slavery, conservative, and radical elements united in some sort, for the purpose of rallying to the national standard to find shelter beneath "the Star-spangled Banner."

The New York East Conference in April, 1861, led by Rev. J. S. Inskip, unanimously declared its unqualified sympathy and support of the government in its defense of the Constitution. In June of the same year the New York Conference followed, led on by the manly report submitted through Rev. J. B. Wakeley, on the State of the Country. In that report was delineated, in unmistakable language, "the formation of the Southern Confederacy ,. . . . its seizure of the forts, mints, custom-houses, vessels, and arms of the United States, . . . and unnatural war against the government." And the report went on and patriotically declared: "No treasure is too costly, no sacrifice too great, no time too long, to put down treason and traitors, and to place our Union on a rock so solid that neither enemies abroad nor traitors at home can move it." Indeed, so arrogant and flagrant had the unpunished crimes of the slave oligarchy become, that the East Baltimore Conference in March, 1862, by a vote of 132 yeas to 15 nays—led on by Revs. A. A. Reese and G. D. Chenoweth—not only expressed its "abhorrence of the rebellion," but declared, "We approve and indorse the present wise and patriotic

Administration, and in the inculcation of loyal principles and sentiments we recognize the pulpit and
press as legitimate instrumentalities."　Not only so,
but the Philadelphia Conference, in March of that
same year, received and unanimously adopted the
report of their Committee on the State of the Country
as presented by the chairman, Rev. Charles Cook,
which affirmed: "We do hereby express our utter
abhorrence and opposition to the present rebellion,
being the offspring of treason, . . . and that
we pledge our influence to encourage and assist the
army and navy, to protect the honor of our flag,
the integrity of the Constituion, and the maintenance of our glorious Union."　The New Jersey
Conference followed with equally patriotic resolutions.

MEMORIALIZING CONGRESS.

As if afraid its influence would not be potent
enough by its General and annual conference action
on the question of slavery, several of the annual
conferences sent up memorials to Congress and to
President Lincoln.　The New York East Conference—when the bill freeing "slaves used for insur-
rectionary purposes" was approved, August 6, 1861,
and another forbidding the return of fugitive slaves
by persons in the army, March 13, 1862, and the abolishment of slavery in the District of Columbia by
Congress, April 16, 1862—adopted a report drawn
up by James Floy, which declared "the system of

American slavery is evidently, in the good providence of God, destined soon to come to an end; that the recent action of our national authorities, by which the nation has been unequivocally committed to the cause of freedom, meets with our entire. approbation." The same body, with the New York Conference, in 1864, memorialized Congress, praying the enactment of an amendment to the Constitution for the abolishment of slavery a year and a half or more before it was done. The New England Conference sent up the following, which, for historic accuracy, prophetic ken, and loyalty to the cause of human freedom, has rarely been surpassed, and will stand in the forefront of the reputation of that conference for level-headedness and right doing. We here reproduce it :

"After thirty years of exciting but healthful agitation on the subject of slavery, the present aspects of our cause furnish abundant motive for devout thanksgiving to God. The two antagonistic tendencies of public sentiment existing and increasing in the nation for so many years, have at length reached their legitimate crisis of mutual and final conflict, of which the issue can not be doubtful. By its own diabolical act [slavery] has been placed in a position where it can claim no constitutional protection, and where there is no prudential motive for its retention; and the voice of the people, which evidently coincides with the voice of God, says: 'Let it perish!' In the Church the progress

of the anti-slavery sentiment has been equally gratifying. Instead of a continued and meager minority
which regarded slavery as a sin, a great majority of
the representative assemblies of the Church register
their solemn verdict of its criminal character, and
demand that it shall cease, not only in the ministry, but in the whole membership."

The Black River Conference also gave no uncertain sound when it declared: "The signs of the
times give evidence that the hitherto dominant
and domineering slave power is rapidly approaching
its end, and even now we may witness its horrible
death-throe. The time is rapidly approaching when
the last fetter will be broken, and the last bondman be released."

Of all the above and many more conferences that
took action in support of the Union, none of them
is more worthy of honor because of the action
taken than the Central Ohio, which adopted resolutions as early as 1861 contemplating a proclamation of emancipation as the only conceivable
solution of our national difficulties. The *Christian
Advocate* of October following, reports the action
taken by said conference at its session in Green-
ville, September 22, 1862:

" *Resolved*, That we believe that the time has
fully come that, from a military necessity for the
safety of the country, such a proclamation should
be made; and we earnestly beseech the President
of the United States to proclaim the emancipation

of all slaves held in the United States, paying loyal men a reasonable compensation for their slaves."

This was, by order of the conference, forwarded to the President of the United States. But before it reached him, as if verifying God's promise, "Call, and while you are calling, I will answer," the President issued September 22, 1862, the Proclamation, to take effect January 1, 1863. This Proclamation was not intended to free all the slaves, but only affected "all persons held as slaves within any State, or any designated part of a State, the people whereof shall be in rebellion against the United States on the first day of January, 1863." Hence it only reached the States of Arkansas, Louisiana—leaving out some parishes—Texas, Mississippi, Alabama, Florida, Georgia, North and South Carolina, and Virginia, in all of which States and parts of States all slaves were henceforth to be free. Other exceptions, such as parts of Virginia, Missouri, Kentucky, West Virginia, Tennessee, Delaware, and Maryland were also included in the above, leaving the slaves in the non-designated parts in slavery.

CHAPTER VII.

THE GENERAL CONFERENCE OF 1864.

ALMOST one year after the Emancipation
Proclamation took effect by reason of the refusal on the part of the South to return to the
Union, the nineteenth session of the General Conference met in the city of Philadelphia. That body
was composed of two hundred and sixteen delegates. Just how any body of men, whether met for
political or religious interests, could properly attend
to affairs, even to the minutiæ, under the then existing circumstances of so exciting character as
those that occurred from May 1; 1864, until the
adjournment of that General Conference, is hard to
conceive. And yet the proceedings of that body
were characterized by patient, wise, and prudent
action. Some of the delegates to that General
Conference had their thoughts, however hard they
strove to prevent it, on Church interests upset, as
they took up the newspapers and found an account
of the atrocious butchery of colored troops at Fort
Pillow by that enemy of the human family, General Forrest. Before leaving the cars upon which
they were traveling, they were startled by the cry
of the newsboys at every station, as they announced

the startling news that the governors of the Western States had offered the United States government eighty-five thousand men for one hundred days, and that the President had accepted the offer; again, that the victory was still in the scales. They had been in session but four days until the wires flashed the news that the irrepressible Grant had crossed the Rapidan in Virginia, and commenced operations in the Wilderness! The next day news came that the armies of the North and South had met in the Wilderness—the former under that invincible hero, and the latter under the intrepid Lee. Since our own Grant was pushing Lee before him nearly everywhere, and knowing how the Church had begun to love General Grant, and that her prayers and influence and sons were with him for the preservation of the Union, it is pretty hard to understand just how that General Conference found time and disposition to work as it did. Its session was during the crisis of the war. As they understood it, "God expects every man to do his best," and they had then an opportunity to view the whole scene, knowing that God himself was interested, since

> "Right forever on the scaffold,
>   Wrong forever on the throne;
> But that scaffold sways the future,
>   And behind the dim unknown
> Standeth God within the shadows,
>   Keeping watch above his own."

So it was on the gory field of battle as well as in that General Conference.

"The conference adopted a new rule on slavery, by a vote of 207 yeas to 9 nays. The small minority of dissenters were delegates from within the then slaveholding States of West Virginia, Maryland, and Kentucky—so that the Methodist Episcopal Church alone, of all the Churches in America, within whose communion slaveholding had been allowed, enacted a prohibitory law abolishing slavery, even within the States where it was allowed to continue by President Lincoln's Proclamation of 1863. Moving forward on the same line, in advance of all the Churches, the same body, already more sweeping in its prohibition of slavery than the civil authorities, yet further anticipated the action of the government in a formal address to the President."

At that General Conference the special Committee appointed on the State of the Country reported as follows:

"The committee have carefully considered the following subject, submitted to them by the General Conference, namely:

"Whereas, It is a well-known fact that the Methodist Episcopal Church was the first to tender its allegiance to the government under the Constitution in the days of Washington; and *whereas,* the fair record of the Church has never been tarnished by disloyalty; and *whereas,* our ministers and people are deeply in sympathy with the government in its efforts to put down rebellion and set the captives free; therefore,

"*Resolved*, That a committee of five be appointed, whose duty it shall be to proceed to Washington to present to the President of these United States the assurances of our Church, in a suitable address, that we are with him in heart and soul in the present struggle for human rights and free institutions.

"The committee, after further consideration of the subject of the delegation it is proposed to send with an address to the President of the United States, beg leave to report that they have instructed their chairman to present, for the approval of the General Conference, the address contemplated in the resolution referred for consideration. The committee still further report that they have nominated as the delegation, Bishop E. R. Ames, Rev. George Peck, Rev. Joseph Cummings, Rev. Charles Elliott, Rev. Granville Moody."

On motion of Thomas C. Golden, seconded by K. P. Jervis, the report was adopted. The committee at once began to prepare the address, and in due time the following was presented:

"To His Excellency, Abraham Lincoln, President of the United States:

"The General Conference of the Methodist Episcopal Church, now in session in the city of Philadelphia, representing nearly seven thousand ministers, and nearly a million of members, mindful of their duty as Christian citizens, take the earliest opportunity to express to you the assurance of the loyalty of the Church, her earnest devotion to the interests of the country, and her sympathy with you in the great responsibilities of your high position in this trying hour.

"With exultation we point to the record of our Church as having never been tarnished by disloyalty. She was the first of the Churches to express, by a deputation of her most distinguished ministers, the promise of support to the government in the days of Washington. In her Articles of Religion she has enjoined loyalty as a duty, and has ever given to the government her most decided support.

"In this present struggle for the nation's life many thousands of her members, and a large number of her ministers, have rushed to arms to maintain the cause of God and humanity. They have sealed their devotion to their country with their blood on every battle-field of this terrible war.

"We regard this dreadful scourge now desolating our land and wasting the nation's life, as the result of a most unnatural, utterly unjustifiable rebellion, involving the crime of treason against the best of human governments, and sin against God. It required our government to submit to its own dismemberment and destruction, leaving it no alternative but to preserve the national integrity by the use of the national resources. If the government had failed to use its power to preserve the unity of the nation and maintain its authority, it would have been justly exposed to the wrath of heaven and to the reproach and scorn of the civilized world. Our earnest and constant prayer is that this cruel and wicked rebellion may be speedily suppressed; and we pledge you our hearty co-operation in all appropriate means to secure this object.

"Loyal and hopeful in national adversity, in prosperity thankful, we most heartily congratulate you on the glorious victories recently gained, and rejoice in the belief that our complete triumph is near.

"We believe that our national sorrows and calamities have resulted, in a great degree, from our forgetfulness of God and oppression of our fellow-men. Chastened by affliction, may the nation humbly repent of her sins, lay aside her haughty pride, honor God in all her future legislation, and render justice to all who have been wronged!

"We honor you for your proclamations of liberty, and rejoice in all the acts of the government designed to secure freedom to the enslaved.

"We trust that when military usages and necessities shall justify interference with established institutions, and the removal of wrongs sanctioned by law, the occasion will be improved, not merely to injure our foes and increase the national resources, but also as an opportunity to recognize our obligations to God and to honor his law. We pray that the time may speedily come when this shall be truly a republican and free country, in no part of which, either State or Territory, shall slavery be known.

"The prayers of millions of Christians, with an earnestness never manifested for rulers before, daily ascend to Heaven that you may be endued with all needed wisdom and power. Actuated by the sentiments of the loftiest and purest patriotism, our prayers shall be continually for the preservation of our country undivided, for the triumph of our cause, and for a permanent peace, gained by sacrifice of no moral principles, but founded on the Word of God, and securing, in righteousness, liberty and equal rights to all.

"Signed in behalf the General Conference of the Methodist Episcopal Church.

"Joseph Cummings, Chairman.
"Philadelphia, May 14, 1864."

To this address the President responded:

"Gentlemen,—In reply to your address, allow me to attest the accuracy of its historical statements, indorse the sentiments it expresses, and thank you in the nation's name for the sure promise it gives.

"Nobly sustained as the government has been by all the Churches, I would utter nothing which might in the least appear invidious against any; yet, without this, it may be fairly said that the Methodist Episcopal Church, not less devoted than the best, is, by its greater numbers, the most important of all. It is no fault in others that the Methodist Church sends more soldiers to the field, more nurses to the hospitals, and more prayers to Heaven, than any. God bless the Methodist Church! Bless all the Churches! And blessed be God, who, in this our great trial, giveth us the Churches!

"A. LINCOLN."

Memorials were sent up to this General Conference, also asking for a colored pastorate and conference organization. Several petitions from the colored members within the District of Columbia and the States of Delaware and Maryland were presented, praying for this. The wisdom of the petitioners is best seen by noting the fact that most of the best work among the colored people within the Church is in the bounds of the territory from whence came most petitions for a colored pastorate and separate conferences. The Church began to see a new door open at the sesame of belching cannons for her admission into the South. She then declared: "As a Church we have never sought, do not now seek, to ignore our duty to the colored population." And besides this, the Church at that conference declared: "Justice to those who have been enslaved requires that in all the privileges of citizenship, as well as in all the other rights of a common manhood, there shall be no distinction founded on color." These were strong words at that early day, and meant what the Church has been teaching ever since. That General Conference created a special committee to look after the interests, hear the appeals, consider what ought to be done by that conference to further the work among the colored members It was known as "the Committee on the State of the Work among the Colored People," to whom all such petitions and memorials were referred. This was not one of the regular standing committees, but a special one appointed for the occasion. After the General Conference had been in possession of. said petitions and memorials two weeks or more, they submitted a report, in which they said that they based their report on "direct information from delegates to the General Conference familiar with the work; from intelligent and trustworthy local preachers who have been deputed by the colored charges in Delaware and Maryland and the District of Columbia to represent them before the committee, and from various memorials setting forth the wishes of our colored members."

That the Church trusted and desired to honor her sable sons, no one doubts. That she was proud of feeling herself loved by them, and an instrument in God's hands of helping to uplift them, is told in the following expression of that conference: "If it be a principle potent to Christian enterprise that the missionary field itself must produce the most efficient missionaries, our colored local preachers are peculiarly important to us at this time." The memorialists were filled with ecstasy when the committee reported the following:

COLORED PASTORATE.

"(1.) Our colored members, ministers, and laymen feel that the times are auspicious to the development of their mental and moral power, and request from us the facilities necessary to this end.

"(2.) A colored pastorate they recognize as among the most important of these facilities, securing to them a ministry adapted to their wants, encouraging their young men to enter the ministerial field, and offering motive and opportunity for general ministerial advancement.

"(3.) They do not, however, propose to secure this by—indeed, they are utterly opposed to—separation from our Church, either with a view to a union with another, or to independent organization. With such a feeling on their part, the General Conference can not consistently with its own responsibility, with their constitutional rights, or with any decent recognition of their loyalty to our Church in all the troubles through which, on their account, she has passed, adopt any measure which shall, even indirectly, look to such a result.

"(4.) Conference organization is asked for from two quarters; other memorials urge that the requests should be granted. The local ministers who have been before us have shown deep solicitude in this direction. . . .

"(7.) From this exhibit of facts two convictions are natural, namely: We must retain the oversight of this people; we must give them efficient colored pastors.

"To retain these pastors as mere local preachers, subject to appointment by white presiding elders, will impair rather than increase their efficiency; will promote congregationalism among them rather than itinerant missionary enterprise.

"To propose their incorporation with the existing annual conferences will be attended with difficulties too formidable every way to be readily disposed of, and the delay incident to such a proposition is incompatible with the urgent requirements of the times.

"In view of these considerations, we recom-mend to the General Conference for adoption the following preamble and resolutions:

"WHEREAS, In the present circumstances of our country, the colored people occupy a position of peculiar interest, appealing to our Christian sympathy, and inviting our missionary enterprise; and

"WHEREAS, This enterprise can not now be made efficient by the policy of our Church hitherto pursued toward them, and especial measures have therefore become necessary; and

"WHEREAS, The exigencies of the case require to efficiency prompt action; therefore, be it

"1. *Resolved*, by the General Conference of the Methodist Episcopal Church in Conference assem-

bled, That it is the duty of our Church to encourage *colored pastorates* for *colored people* wherever
practicable, and to contribute to their efficiency by
every means in our power.

"*Resolved*, That the efficiency of said pastorates
can be best promoted by distinct conference organizations, and that therefore the bishops be, and they
are hereby, authorized to organize among our
colored ministers, for the benefit of our colored
members and population, mission conferences—one
or more—where, in their godly judgment, the exigencies of the work may demand it, and, should
more than one be organized, to determine their
boundaries until the meeting of the next General
Conference, said conference or conferences to possess
all the powers usual to mission annual conferences:
Provided, that nothing in this resolution be so
construed as to impair the existing constitutional
rights of our colored members on the one hand, or
to forbid, on the other, the transfer of white ministers to said conference or conferences where it
may be practicable and deemed necessary.

"3. *Resolved*, That our General Missionary
Committee be requested to take into careful consideration the condition of our colored people, and
should conferences be organized among them, make
to them—consistently with other demands upon its
funds—such appropiations as may be essential to
success."

Annual or mission conferences being composed

of traveling preachers, it was necessary that some colored local preachers be admitted into the traveling connection before they could be formed into a conference, which gave rise to a question upon which the same committee made a report, which was adopted, as follows (Jour. 1864, p. 253):

"We, the committee to whom this subject was finally referred, beg leave to report that we are not aware of any legal obstacle to the reception of colored preachers into our annual conferences."

This General Conference at a later day made more specific and direct provision for the Delaware and Washington Conferences in the following resolution (Jour. 1864, p. 263):

"The Washington Conference shall embrace Western Maryland, the District of Columbia, Virginia, and the territory south.

"The Delaware Conference shall embrace the territory north and east of the Washington Conference.

"*Resolved,* That in order to constitute the first conferences of colored members, the rule of Discipline requiring a probation of two years, be so far suspended as to allow the bishops to organize into one or more annual conferences such colored local elders as have traveled two or more years under a presiding elder, and shall be recommended by a quarterly conference, and by at least ten elders who are members of an annual conference."

The Delaware Conference was organized July

28, 1864, and the Washington Conference October 27, 1864. It will be noted that "the constitutional rights of our colored members" were recognized, as well as the difficulties of incorporating the work.

Let us now examine the above resolutions more closely.

Blessings seldom come unattended. At a glance any one can see that the requests of the colored members had been granted. Henceforth they were to have (1) colored pastorates, the very thing for which they had prayed. No one doubts, we think, that the granting of that very thing gave birth to all the other race questions that do or may arise touching the relations of the two races within the Church. The wisdom of that General Conference peered away out into the future. It probably saw a time when advanced ideas would lead men within the Church to advanced work. These pastorates created by that General Conference were to be for "colored people." They were to be allowed (2) separate conferences. There was no way to avoid them where there were "colored pastorates for colored people." Just so. These separate conferences, however, were (3) "not to impair existing rights of our colored members, nor yet (4) to forbid the transfer of white ministers to said conferences where it may be practicable and deemed necessary." What "existing rights" had colored members? To remain in any Church they chose within Methodism, or join with and worship in any congregation within the Methodist Episcopal Church. It did not stop there, but action was taken looking to the education of the race. The General Conference Committee on Education reported as follows:

"The committee have had before them the memorial of Rev. J. F. Wright in reference to the Wilberforce University, and, in view of its peculiar character and relation to the Church, we offer for adoption the following resolution:

"*Resolved*, That we heartily sympathize with the noble purpose contemplated in the establishment of Wilberforce University and we do hereby earnestly commend the institution to the prayers and liberal contributions of the friends of humanity."

Just what "the peculiar character and relation" were, is not stated. It may have been that the enterprise was sprung upon the Church before it had been duly authorized. It may have been that its "peculiar character and relation" meant that it was to be exclusively colored. It makes no difference as to what was meant, some way or other that institution soon passed into other hands.

Again, it would have been folly to grant separate conferences for the colored membership and leave standing the old rule, and allow it to apply in this case, requiring a probation of two years before being admitted to an annual conference. This was brought forward at once, and the animus of the General Conference on the subject was at once manifested by the following resolution:

BENNETT SEMINARY, GREENSBORO, N. C.

"*Resolved*, That in order to constitute the first conference of colored members, the rule of the Discipline requiring a probation of two years be so far suspended as to allow the bishops to organize into one or more annual conferences such colored local elders as have traveled two or more years under a presiding elder and shall be recommended by a quarterly conference and by at least ten elders who are members of an annual conference."

This was a wise and prudential action. Wise in that it at once dissipated any thought that might have arisen in the minds of the less stable members, that the matter was simply put in a complicated shape to keep the colored members at bay, and thereby eventually drive out of the Methodist Episcopal Church all the colored people. To have kept them waiting under the probationary rule would probably have done much harm. Prudential in that even the local elders were to come up well recommended: (1) By their own people, among whom they lived and worked, and who therefore could testify as to their moral, religious, and literary fitness for the traveling connection. (2) To be recommended "by at least ten elders (white) who are members of an annual conference." Who were better qualified than such elders to know who were and who were not qualified for traveling preachers—our own people had no experience in matters of that kind—in that they would naturally be able and more willing to speak against those "wolves in sheep's clothing" who sometimes "climb up some other way" into our annual conferences for the purpose of fleecing, instead of feeding, the flock of God? Our own people might have been in some way related to the applicants or ignorant of their devices. Why should not some precautions be observed when clothing with authority those who, even then, must have been witnessing "the pains, the groans, the dying strife" of an institution that had grown gray in crime and debauchery—under which for two hundred and forty-four years the race had suffered in more ways than the Hebrews in Egypt? They had never enjoyed even the privilege of elementary training in any way fitting them for happiness and usefulness in the world. They were poor and ignorant. Poor in that even the good name of the race was gone; and who does not know that a

"Good name, in man and woman, ...
  Is the immediate jewel of their souls?
  Who steals my purse steals trash; 'tis something, nothing;
  'Twas mine, 'tis his, and has been slave to thousands;
  But he that filches from me my good name
  Robs me of that which not enriches him,
  And makes me poor indeed."

We do not know that additional weight attaches to the above by knowing that Shakespeare put these words into the mouth of Iago; but it is a fair statement of the condition of the race when the Emancipation Proclamation was issued. The morality of the race under the old *régime* is the prodigy·

of the age! And yet they knew nothing theoretically of morality, and had opportunities for but *few examples of it.* They knew nothing of home economics, and not five in one hundred of the rank and file could count correctly ten dollars in small change. Hence the Church was wise in throwing around this people safeguards as well as charity. They knew but little, if anything, of the comforts of home life, the proper training of children; while the fantastic mode of dressing immediately after the war tells a tale at which a heathen should blush. They knew comparatively nothing either of Church polity or moral science. Those who have found occasion to laugh at the huge mistakes of some of our ministers, as well as some others who had enjoyed better opportunities, must find a sufficient explanation in the previous condition of the race. Was the Methodist Church not right in doing as it did?

CHAPTER VIII.

THE BEGINNING OF A GREAT WORK.

THE beginning of a work among these images of God cut in ebony is found in the following resolutions looking to the protection of the interests of the colored man by the civil government. It is nothing against a system that it was badly managed or fell into bad hands, or else our venerated Constitution is involved. That General Conference (1864) in its report on freedmen, said:

"(1) *Resolved*, That in the events which have thrown the thousands of freed people upon the benevolence of the humane and loyal people of the North, we recognize a providential call to the Christian public for contributions for their physical relief and mental and moral elevation and especially to the Church of Christ for the means of their evangelization.

"(2) *Resolved*, That the best interests of the freedmen of the country demand legislation that shall foster and protect this people, and we do hereby respectfully but *earnestly urge* upon Congress the importance of establishing, as soon as practicable, a Bureau of Freedmen's Affairs, as contemplated in the bills now pending."

What did this mean? If it meant anything, the

Church meant to practice, at its earliest convenience, the doctrine it had been preaching for the last eighty years and more,—that the poor enslaved colored man should be properly trained to enjoy this life and that which is to come. It meant that just as soon as the alarms of war had sufficiently subsided and God opened the way, or signified that an entrance could be gained, to go at once up and down through the Southland carrying the gospel of free salvation to the down-trodden, poverty-stricken, and demoralized colored man. While but few, if any, believe the only mission of the Methodist Episcopal Church in the South was to the poor colored man, but few will doubt that, had it no other call to go into the South, that were enough. But few rational Christians believe the Church had no call into the South.

That the Church was needed there, no one will question when the condition of the colored man at that time is considered, as well as the relation the Methodist Episcopal Church, South, sustained to the colored man before and during the war, and that other significant fact that the colored man, as such, was, and for that matter is, peculiarly either a Baptist or a Methodist. From the beginning Methodism took hold of him, and he learned that, wherever found, a true Methodist was his friend. This in itself is sufficient explanation of the peculiarity referred to above. What was the condition of the colored man at the close of the war? When the black smoke of battle arose from a hundred battle-fields the entire colored population—four and a half millions—came forth ignorant, superstitious, degraded, and poverty-stricken. The only beam of hope rested entirely on the education of the race. The emancipation was followed by the enfranchisement of these ignorant and superstitious people. The cry of opposition was heard vociferously in the South, while in some places in the North leading newspapers and men expressed doubts as to the wisdom of the thing. Who, under the then existing circumstances, doubted the earnestness of those who cried out as they saw the colored men clothed with freedom and franchise, yet slaves to superstition and ignorance:

> " A poor, blind Samson is in our land,
>   Bound hand and foot, and prone upon his back;
>   But who knows that, in some drunken revel,
>   He may rise and grasp the pillars
>   Of our temple's liberties, shake the foundations
> ' Till all beneath its broken columns lie in ruins?"

Amid the religious training received from that part of the Methodist Episcopal Church, South, that trained them at all, did not appear anything different from the system of slavery in vogue, save the promise of an eternal Sabbath. It is true a colored membership was reported by the Methodist Episcopal Church, South; but this did not mean that the colored people within that Church were permitted to worship God in their own congregations, or that there were any colored pastors or class-leaders among that membership. If slavery had continued, the condition of the colored man religiously could never have become better. Just how—unless force of circumstances played a part in the drama—a brotherly feeling could have arisen or existed in the bosom of the poor colored man under that *régime*, we can not, for the life of us, surmise. But all that was ended with the war, and still there was but little, if any, change. The withdrawals at first opportunity of colored people from the Methodist Episcopal Church, South, meant something. The Methodist Episcopal Church, South, was then, at any rate, unwilling to educate the colored man. In proof of the last assertion, we turn to page 148 of Dr. A. G. Haygood's book, "Our Brother in Black." The following, published in 1881 by this leading philosopher and clergyman in the Methodist Episcopal Church, South, is as significant as sound. He says:

"If the work of educating the Negroes of the South is ever to be carried on satisfactorily, if ever the best results are to be accomplished, then *Southern white people must take part in the work of teaching Negro schools.* There have been some very sad and hurtful mistakes in the relations assumed by most of us of the South to this whole matter, and especially in the fact that, with very rare exceptions, our people have steadfastly refused to teach Negro children, especially since they were made free, for love or money. They have recoiled from Negro schools as if there were personal degradation in teaching them. Perhaps the state of things that existed at the South for a full decade after the war, and for which Southern people were not alone responsible—a state of things that made it impracticable for Southern white men and women to teach Negro schools—was inevitable. But so it was; they could not do it without 'losing caste.' As I am trying to state facts honestly, I should add, the prevailing sentiment of the South would not even now look favorably upon such teachers; but I must say we are growing in sense as well as grace on this subject."

Without further comment, the above corroborates the statement that the condition of the freedmen in the South directly after the war, temporally, spiritually, morally, and intellectually, was a loud enough call, and the mission of enough importance to warrant the action of the General Conference of 1864 in its action that virtually announced the intention of the Methodist Episcopal Church to go into the South. The fact that conferences had been opened in the South for colored people was sufficient proof.

THE CHURCH IN THE SOUTH.

When the General Conference of 1868 met in the city of Chicago, Ill., for its twentieth session, among other things it took up the subject of the relation of the Church to the colored man. There were present at that General Conference two hundred and forty-three delegates. When the General Conference of 1864 authorized the formation of mission conferences in the South for colored people, as a Church, it "had been practically excluded for twenty years" from Alabama, North and South Carolina, Georgia, Florida, Tennessee, Mississippi, Louisiana, Arkansas, and Texas, while a generation had grown up under the immediate care, as it were, of the Methodist Episcopal Church, South. It is true that the Methodist Episcopal Church had held on in some sort in the city of Baltimore—this being her strongest fort—while through some parts of Delaware, Maryland, Virginia, Kentucky, and Missouri it had a foothold. Our Church in 1863, in the last-named States, claimed 332 effective preachers, 84,673 members, and 919 church-buildings. By the next year, when the General Conference of 1864 met for its nineteenth session in Philadelphia, it claimed in the above-named five slave States 309 effective preachers, 87,072 members—15,898 being colored—and 982 churches, being an increase in these five States of 2,399 members, not including probationers, and a decrease of 23 effective preachers, and an increase of 63 church-buildings. Thus it may be seen that a wise Providence proclaimed the mission of our Church; and there was then, as we see now, no mistake made on the part of our Church when it heard and obeyed the commission in this case, "Go ye into all the world, and preach the gospel to every creature." The crowning act touching the subject we discuss was given by the General Conference of 1864 in these words: "We are not aware of any legal obstacle to the reception of colored preachers into our annual conferences." Touching the work done by the last General Conference, and showing somewhat of the results attained, the Bishops' Address to the Twentieth General Conference contained the following:

"They [the Delaware and Washington colored conferences] now contain one hundred and one ministers and twenty-six thousand four hundred and eighty-seven members and probationers. The creation of these conferences was hailed by our colored ministers and membership with great joy, and has, we believe, been productive of much good. The ministers are becoming familiar with the mode of conducting business, and many of them are rapidly improving. At their recent sessions they elected representatives to this body according to the form of the Discipline for electing delegates. Whether these representatives should be admitted, you alone have authority to decide. In our judgment, the success of this work demands all the encouragement which the General Conference can properly give."

The regular and natural succession of action touching the relation of the Church toward the colored man seems to declare, to our mind at any rate, that it has the divine sanction. The submission of the above resolution brought at once before the General Conference of 1868 the question of the advisability of admitting—not colored testimony, or testimony from people of color—but colored delegates to equality in the General Conference of one of the largest denominations in the world. The Christ-like spirit of the bishops in presenting the matter, supported by their modest indorsement of it, was manly. They said: "In our judgment, the success of this work demands all the encouragement which the General Conference can properly give." It may have been that it was not thoroughly settled in the minds of all the delegates of that General Conference. The result, however, was satisfactory, in that James Davis and Benjamin Brown were seated as delegates, and thereby the equal rights of our colored members were not only recognized, but everything looking to their elevation, done by the Church, was stamped with approval. The adjournment of that General Conference did not take place until provision for other conferences for our people, at their own request, was made. The year preceding that General Conference a colored presiding elder had been appointed over a district in Kentucky; nine mission conferences had been organized in our Southern field; colored preachers had been received into the Kentucky and Missouri Annual Conferences. Notwithstanding this, wherever a mission conference was organized a new inspiration seemed to overshadow the entire work. The provision above referred to was as follows:

"'*Resolved*, 1. That the bishops who may preside in the Kentucky Conference during the next four years, are hereby authorized to organize the colored ministers within the bounds of said conference into a separate annual conference, if said ministers request it; and if, in the judgment of the bishops, the interest of the work requires it, to be called the ———— Conference: *Provided*, that nothing in this resolution shall be construed to impair the existing constitutional rights of our colored members on the one hand, or, on the other, to forbid the transfer of white ministers to said conference, whenever it may be deemed desirable or expedient.'

"So soon as this resolution was taken up, a motion was made to lay it upon the table, which was lost.

"A motion to amend by inserting, '*Provided*, that colored members may remain in the Kentucky Conference,' was laid on the table.

"A motion to strike out the words 'the interest of the work,' and insert 'the unity and success of the Church,' was laid on the table; and the resolution was adopted as matured by the Committee on Boundaries."

The motions subsequently made show at once the animus of the white brethren of that conference at that time. While many were anxious to have restrictions, others objected to it *in toto*. But, as in the General Conference, so it has been in nearly every annual conference, that a wide difference of opinion on the color-line question existed. It is well that it was so.

Following hard upon the above action in the interest of the colored man, this General Conference paid special attention to its work so grandly begun in the sunny South. While the discussion of the status of the colored delegates elicited much animation, the restrictions were removed from the conferences of the Church in the South, irrespective of color, by a vote of 197 to 15. All our benevolent societies were instructed to redouble their diligence to meet the exigencies of the case; our Book Concerns were to publish one or more papers adapted to the new order of things within the South; transfers, if needed, were to be sent into this fruitful field; training-schools and theological schools were ordered for the special training of the colored people of the South within our Church and without, if accepted. The bishops were requested to give the colored work special episcopal supervision. As a finale of the action of that General Conference, an "enabling act" for the establishment of the third annual conference among our colored members was passed, with the provision that in every case the *rights* of every preacher were to be fully and carefully, as well as impartially, considered. The white preachers and teachers who were sent by the Church into the South to carry out this plan of work were, in too many cases, not only subjected to insult, but cruel scourgings and false imprisonment, as if ostracism was not cruel and wicked punishment enough. But many of those thus treated were men and women of God, and therefore consistent but firm and true heroes and heroines.

Dr. Walden (now bishop), in an address, Aug. 13, 1883, at the anniversary of the Freedmen's Aid Society, spoke of this work. The following needs no comment, as he speaks of the period in our work in the South at which we now are, and we insert it here as a retrospect:

" Two courses were open—one to delay employing colored preachers until they could be educated, the other to put these untutored men to work at once. No people ever needed the gospel more than did the freed people. Standing in the midst of new relations, the possessors of a new-found freedom for which they had never been trained, they needed both the restraints and the inspiration of the gospel. The Wesleyan prescience of our Church recognized this need, and at the same time the fact that these unlearned preachers, if divinely called, could so tell the story of the Cross as to benefit their people. The lives of many of these men had been an unbroken period of slave-toil; but the sequel proves that they knew enough of the saving power of Christ and the fullness of his love to instruct their hearers in the way of life, and we now see that their relation to this work was not unlike to that of the first of Wesley's lay preachers to their work among their own classes in England.

"With this illustration before us of the general principle that a people may and must be instrumental in their own evangelization, let us study some of the results of our itinerant system among the freedmen—of our itinerancy and its auxiliary agencies. All understand our itinerancy to be the general superintendency and the pastorate; by auxiliary agencies I mean our sub-pastorate, in which the class-leaders stand, our Church literature, and our Sunday-schools. The mere suggestion of the fact leads you at once to see that the real function of each and all of these is to re-enforce both the general and the particular work committed to the itinerancy or three foldpastorate—the bishops, presiding elders, and pastors of our Church. The very fact of taking this comprehensive system to a people who had no system, of beginning at once to build them up into it, could not be without producing some marked and favorable results. I mention the more obvious of these:

"(a) The freedmen who were recognized as having a call to preach could do little more than exhort, but they were put into the pastoral relation; a great Church committed to them a new and solemn trust, and laid upon them grave responsibilities; they were under the leadership of the superintendents of the missions—good, prudent, self-sacrificing men—men who in their devotion to duty represented the highest life of their Church. Such things could not be without affecting these untutored preachers. Crude as all they did may have been at first, their pastorate benefited the people they served, and was to themselves a means of training, of real and rapid progress; and there are still in the effective ranks of the conferences which came from such beginnings many pious, able, and successful preachers, who were thus transferred from the cotton and rice fields and sugar plantations to, and trained in, our itinerant ministry.

"(*b*) As the work progressed, these colored men acquired by observation and experience, and such study as was possible with them, a wider knowledge of their work; and in due course the bishops began to appoint some of them as presiding elders, investing them with all the honors and responsibilities of this important office. It should also be stated that the Church that acted thus through her bishops was constantly displaying to them an encouraging interest in them by furnishing means to aid in the support of their Church work.

"(*c*) In the annual conferences they were and are brought under the presidency of our bishops—the most efficient presiding officers in this or any other country, a fact that became most obvious at the Ecumenical Methodist Conference. The very methods of business in our annual conferences, and the promptness with which it is dispatched under this presidency, have had such influence on the older conferences that the advantages of like administration to the colored conferences are obvious. The influence of the conference session ought also to be named, as these annual meetings of the preachers have all along affected most favorably the character of Methodism. These colored preachers have been coming together, as do their brethren in older conferences, to report and review the year's work, to pass upon the character of each one, to consider the various connectional and benevolent causes, to attend to all the business that is usually presented, and to enjoy the social privileges and religious services to which all our preachers look forward with deep interest. Every such session tends to make them wiser and more effective in their work.

"(d) Under our system of study for probationers and deacons, the colored preachers are steadily improving, and their conferences are becoming more careful as to the qualifications of those who are received into the ministry. I well remember the class taken on trial in the South Carolina Conference in 1867; near a dozen of them were then uncouth and ill-clad men, who seemed to have come direct from the plantations; little or nothing was said as to even elementary education; they were taken as they were, and sent out to do work for the Master, who ordaineth strength even out of the mouths of babes. But it is radically different in that conference now; at its session, last January, I heard the report of examinations, and learned thereby that the standard of qualification is applied more rigidly each succeding year. I rejoiced in this as a fact common to all these colored conferences; and yet I also rejoiced to remember that when the exigencies required it, our Church dared to send out the earlier members of that and other conferences, illiterate as they were, to the work of winning souls.

"(e) These early colored preachers, coming as they did from a condition in which there was no home, in the better sense of that word, soon came to know something of the importance that our Church attaches to Sunday-schools. They were organized, often in the crudest form; but they have been improved, and now nearly two thousand are reported in the twelve conferences. This work is important there, not only because it is in behalf of the youth and children, but also because there has been, and is, a relatively great demand for such work in the South. It is a fact that the ratio between the number of Sunday-school scholars and Church members of any and all Protestant denominations in the South is far below what it is in the North. The schools organized in our "new Southern field" have been aided with papers published by our Church, and especially adapted to the condition of the scholars. All the teachers employed by the Freedmen's Aid Society have done good and faithful service in these Sunday-schools. Through them the Church has been, and is, furnishing moral and mental instruction to about one hundred thousand of the youth and children, that will be of incalculable value to them, and through them to the Church and the nation.

"(*f*) The Methodist newspapers published in the South—within this new field—by our Church, in order to furnish a literature specially adapted to the condition and needs of the people, have been potent for good. We may not be able to estimate the force of the fact that papers have been provided for them which they in a special sense regarded as their own. It was no mean fact with them that a part of the capital of the Book Concern was being employed to publish papers which, by their very location, must chiefly be for them. And the presence of a depository of books at Atlanta tended to impress the lesson, taught in so many ways, that our Church was ready and anxious to help them in their every effort to reach the plane of a higher and better life.

"Other facts might be named to show how every thing that is forceful in our itinerancy and its auxiliary agencies has been constantly, wisely, and effectively employed to reach, evangelize and elevate these colored people. It has been more than a formal recognition of Christian equality; it has been the continuous presence and power of educational relations as well as educational agencies among them. The Church, during these years, has recognized the divine call into her ministry of more than a thousand of these men, thereby reposing a confidence and conferring an honor that has been a special inspiration to them, and, in good degree, to their people. Ministerial position and pastoral duties, prerogatives and responsibilities, shared in common with the largest corps of preachers in our country, have been made realities to them. When that whole people shall come to the plane and glory of a true manhood and womanhood, it will be known that the impartial planting of our system of itinerancy among them was one of the early and potent means of their elevation.

"3. The aim of the Methodist Episcopal Church is to enlist every local society in the support of her benevolent enterprises. She would give to every person converted at her altars the opportunity to do work for the Master. For this reason, all her pastors are charged with the duty of presenting to their congregations the claims of the Missionary, Church Extension, Freedmen's Aid, Sunday-school, Tract, and Educational causes, and of affording to all the opportunity to contribute thereto according to their ability. Into each sphere of work represented by these causes, the Church has been led by a marked providence, and her efforts in them have been attended with her Lord's signal favor. The presentation of these causes in the relation they hold to the world's evangelization, the end for which Christ established his Church, teaches with special emphasis the magnitude of her mission, and indicates the certainty of ultimate success. How the faith of God's people has enlarged under the inspiration of this widening work! These causes have been presented more or less fully to our new societies in the South.

"The colored preachers and people have taken a ready interest in the Missionary Society because it carried the gospel to them. The preachers were not learned, and the people were poor; but what if the earlier missionary sermons were crude presentations of a world-wide cause? what if but a few pennies were collected in a charge? the people were thus coming into contact with the genius of the gospel, and beginning to have some part in the movement that is conquering the world. Among the many wise things done during the administration of the revered Dr. Durbin as missionary secretary, the one of all others that has affected and will continue to affect our Church the most, was providing for the organization of the Sunday-schools into missionary societies; wise and potential, because thus, in a practical and methodical way, the idea of the world's evangelization is fixed in the thought of the youth and children, by far the greatest idea touching the human race that can be given to the human mind.

"The colored preachers have been learning this fundamental idea of the missionary cause and the purpose of each of the other benevolences of our Church, and in their own way it may be presenting them to their people; but the result has been a measure of enlightenment in these directions, an increasing knowledge of the far-reaching plans of the Church to which they belong, a clearer consciousness that by being brought within her pale they have part in one of the great aggressive Christian movements of the age. Standing as they do in the dawn of a new day, this conscious identification with all the benevolent plans of the Church that brought them the gospel can not do less than enlarge their views of Christian duty, and inspire them with zeal for and devotion to causes grand in themselves and glorious in their results.

"4. The preaching that is distinctively Methodistic has had its influence in this, as in other fields. While we hold the fundamental truths of Christianity in common with other evangelical Churches—points of agreement, each of which is infinitely more important than all the questions in regard to which there is a difference—all do not place the same emphasis we do on some of these truths. Our preachers in the 'new Southern field,' as elsewhere, have given special prominence to the willingness and power of Jesus to save every one who comes to him; the universal call and the gracious ability of every one to come; the radical character of the change wrought in conversion—a new life through divine power; the adoption into the divine family, and that adoption clearly, satisfactorily attested through the witness of the Holy Spirit; the complete cleansing power of the blood of Christ, and the keeping power of the promised grace. Need I say in this presence that the emphasis given to these Scriptural doctrines by our ministry has molded the experience of Methodists in every society, and made the meeting for testimony, whether love-feast or class-meeting, a part of our Church life?

The preaching of these doctrines in the earnest Methodist way among the colored people, the building up of a Church among them under the molding and inspiring effect of such truths, the leading of the members up to a clear, well-defined religious experience, is giving them a Church life, the advantage of which is best known from what Methodism has done for other peoples. Already the advance of Christian morality, the growing habits of industry and economy, the increasing spirit of benevolence and liberality, the new home-life where home was so recently unknown—the fruits of an evangelical gospel faithfully preached—show what we have done, and are the promise and pledge of a pure, strong, and active Church in every part of our new Southern field in the near future."

CHAPTER IX.

THE COLORED BISHOP QUESTION.

THE quadrennium from 1868 to 1872 exhibited a marvelous growth among the colored membership of the Methodist Episcopal Church. This was but the pulsation started by Methodism among her hitherto downtrodden children, by her labor of love in carrying to them the gospel of free salvation through the agency of her benevolent societies, the class of bishops, General Conference officers, and the consecrated and self-denying white teachers from the North, who left their homes of comfort and joy to go South and put themselves upon God's altar for the elevation, morally, financially, intellectually, and spiritually, of their "brother in black." The work done, and its effects in so short a time, seem now the marvel of the age! The scattered sheep had been gathered from the hills and valleys, the cane-brakes and swamps, from the villages and the larger cities, into societies nearly everywhere. Wherever possible they had been organized into conferences as had been provided by the action of the General Conference of 1864. With the application for recognition came that also for separate conferences. Two separate annual conferences had been organized before 1865—the Delaware Conference, July 28, 1864, and the Washington Conference, October 27, 1864. Besides this, the Rule of the Discipline, requiring a probation of two years, had been suspended so far as to permit our bishops to organize annual conferences with such colored local elders as had traveled two or more years under a presiding elder, who were recommended by a quarterly conference and by at least ten white elders. Thus the constitutional rights of the colored membership of the Church had been recognized, and the marvelous growth among them during this quadrennium was but a manifestation of appreciation on the part of the religious colored people of the South, evidence of their preference for Methodism, pure and simple.

The fact that colored delegates were recognized by the General Conference of 1868, and provision made for the organization of the Lexington Annual Conference, that had hitherto been mixed with the Kentucky Conference, white; that separate annual conferences had been formed; indeed, that every practically conceivable thing was being done by the Church for her colored members,—caused many to flock toward her that had fled for safety in another direction. The tide was soon checked by the ministry and membership of the two colored denominations—the African Zion and the African Methodist Churches—that were toiling in the same field, by crying out "the Methodist Episcopal Church will never permit a colored man to be elected a bishop." Consternation seized many of our members when they were told that the Methodist Episcopal Church would only tolerate a black membership as "hewers of wood and drawers of water." It at last became to many, as they said, "self-evident, that to retain the better class of colored people there must be no discrimination anywhere in Methodism on account of race, color, or previous condition of servitude." Many, many hard battles were fought, not with the enemy of souls, but with our brethren of the above-named two denominations. From 1868 to the adjournment of the General Conference of 1872 a bitter religious warfare was waged. At last, as the quadrennium drew to a close, it was evident that the agitation of the question of a bishop of African descent had not only done much injury, poisoning and unsettling the minds of our colored membership, but that, in one way or the other, the question must be put and answered by the ensuing General Conference. This was one of the most important questions considered by the General Conference of 1872, sitting in Brooklyn, New York. This, the twenty-first session of our General Conference, will be remembered as the largest ever held by our Church up to that time, there being four hundred and twenty-one delegates. Several of our colored conferences sent up memorials in favor of the election of a bishop of African descent. As they were presented they were respectfully referred to the Committee on

15

Episcopacy, composed of one delegate from each annual conference, colored or white. The petition for a bishop of African descent from the preachers' meeting of New Orleans received the following reply:

"The special committee to which was referred the memorial of the New Orleans preachers' meeting of May 23d, asking for the election of an additional bishop, who shall be of African descent, respectfully report: That at a meeting of the committee, held May 30th, the statements of the memorialists and their requests were carefully considered. The very reasonable demand, that at least some action may be taken which shall assure our people that the Methodist Episcopal Church invites to her altars peoples of every nation, and extends to them equal rights in her worship and government, was responded to with great unanimity by the following declaration of facts which, we are persuaded, will be entirely satisfactory to the memorialists."

Then follows the report of the Committee on Episcopacy, viz.:

"The Committee on Episcopacy report to the General Conference concerning the election of a colored bishop: (1) That they are deeply impressed with the Christian spirit manifested by those memorializing the General Conference on this subject. The rapid progress our brethren of color are making in all that elevates mankind is most commendable, and we have no doubt there is a future of great promise before them. Your committee would further report that, in their judgment, there is nothing in race, color, or former condition that is a bar to an election to the episcopacy, the true course being for us to elect only such persons as are, by their pre-eminent piety, endowments, culture, general fitness, and acceptability best qualified to fill the office. (2) The claims of our numerous and noble-hearted membership of African descent to a perfect equality of relations with all others in our communion are fully recognized by the Discipline, and amply demonstrated in the administration of the Methdist Episcopal Church. There is no word 'white' to discriminate against race or color known in our legislation; and being of African descent does not prevent membership with white men in annual conferences, nor ordination at the same altars, nor appointment nor eligibility to the highest office in the Church. (3) Election to the office of bishop from among candidates who are mutually equal can not be determined on the ground of color or any other special consideration. It can only be by fair and honorable competition between the friends of the respective candidates. And yet the presentation of a well-qualified man of African descent would, doubtless, secure very general support in view of the great interests of the Church, which would thereby be more abundantly promoted. No such opportunity, however, has been. afforded at this General Conference."

Quite a while before the assembling of that General Conference the colored bishop question had been widely discussed, receiving very general consideration and favorable mention in some localities. It, however, was not of a demonstrative character. The fair, plain, Christian statements of that General Conference put an end to the "color question" within the Church, *so far as special ecclesiastical legislation goes.* May we not hope that it put a quietus upon those without the Church who prefer to arrogate to themselves a kind of aristocratical attitude, because they have solved the Negro problem by divorce, but who willingly join in any outcry that will have a tendency to condone any action relating to "the vexed question" they have taken, or seem to shadow any spirit of unkindness that would naturally attach to such a wicked divorce? The manliness, Christian spirit, and unwavering fidelity of the Methodist Episcopal Church toward the colored man from his arrival in this country, so far as the heart of the Church is concerned, ought to be "read and known of all men." That General Conference said all on the colored bishop question that could be said; and, for that matter, all on the race question that needs to be said for all time to come.

While glancing backward and beholding what the Methodist Episcopal Church has done, and is now doing, for the amelioration of the condition and giving the colored man in general, and the colored membership within the communion of the Church in particular, prestige, we feel as if the ignorance of any colored man in this country who dares say the Church, as such, has not loved and respected the race, is inexcusable, reprehensible, and hate-provoking. In many instances the Church did not do what we asked; in others it did not do what others thought it should have done; but time and experience have taught us it did generally what was best. It was feared that much harm would come to Methodism among our people if a bishop of African descent were not chosen at that General Conference. Ought we to say it was the hope of some? In the rural districts, where the general intelligence of the race was not above par, it may have caused friction because of the omnipresence of "colored bishops," "General Conference officers," "college presidents," etc. The years that are to come, unless a strange influence not related to that of the Church of the past comes upon our Methodism, will show that up to this time it was better as it happened. The election of a man of African descent was urged and expected: (1) To tighten our hold upon our people by offsetting outside statements that the Church would never elect a colored man to the bishopric; (2) To remove any lingering doubts, if there remained any, as to the intention of the Church touching the relation of the colored man to it. We doubt not many, without the Church, who persistently *pushed* this matter, urging it through their Church papers, the secular press, and in nearly every public place, and on nearly every occasion; who did this for the specific purpose of demoralizing and scattering our membership, though done with a seeming gravity and earnestness worthy of a better cause, did not honestly believe it possible that the great Methodist Episcopal Church would even go as far as it did; believing that it was an impossibility, as much so as it would be to elect a *white* man to the bishopric in one of the distinctively colored organizations, were there the same number of white people within the communion of those three Churches, comparatively, that there are colored in our Church, and that the Church would not only passively refuse, but would plainly say so. This would naturally have weakened their faith, and they would have doubted the sincerity of the professions of the Church made in favor of the colored man by it in the past. On the contrary, the action of that General Conference *had no such effect* where the truth of the matter was properly told, or where the intelligence of our people made them conversant with the past history of the Church on the color-line question.

The discussion of the question was kept up until the assembling of the session of the *General Conference of* 1876. Without stopping to speak of the spirit manifested in the discussion of this question, pro and con, outside of the General Conference, nor to speak our views then or now, wishing to give as complete an account of the manner in which that General Conference was brought to see this question, we simply state that the discussion was carried into nearly, if not every congregation in the Church during the quadrennium. The whole matter, phœnix-like, came to the surface at the call for resolutions and memorials. The Mississippi Conference led with the following, presented by Moses Adams:

"WHEREAS, The Methodist Episcopal Church has under her care one hundred and fifty thousand members of African descent; and *whereas*, the said Church meets with great opposition from other Methodist bodies, I therefore respectfully ask this General Conference to elect a man of African descent to the office of bishop in the Methodist Episcopal Church. This is asked for two reasons: (1) That the Church needs one to help defend' her cause. Nothing, in my judgment, would build up the Methodist Episcopal Church more than the election of a bishop from the membership of African descent. (2) The race is not fully represented in the Methodist Episcopal Church without one such being elected to that high office of trust."

From the West Virginia Conference the following was presented by G. W. Atkinson:

"*Resolved*, That the Committee on Episcopacy consider the expediency of electing a German bishop and one or more African bishops, to supervise the German and African conferences of the Methodist Episcopal Church in America."

The Delaware Conference sent up a memorial in favor of the election of a bishop of African descent, which was presented by H. Jolley. The petition in favor of the same sent up from the Georgia Conference was presented by Rev. C. O. Fisher, signed by himself and sixteen others. The Mississippi Conference sent up a similar petition by A. C. McDonald. The foregoing gives a faint idea of the scope of the question.

Just how that General Conference would handle the question, striking the happy, golden mean between the two extremes, without reflecting upon the past history of the Methodist Episcopal Church relating to the colored membership on the one hand, or, if necessary to refuse, how it could avoid injuring the work already established among the race, was a perplexing question. Each memorial was given a careful and respectful investigation and promptly and properly referred to the Committee on Episcopacy. At last, after many guesses and prophecies by friends of the measure, and others, the work of the Committee on Episcopacy was finished. When the committee signified its readiness to report, on motion of General Clinton B. Fisk, Report No. 2 of the Committee on Episcopacy was taken up. When the secretary arose to read it, it appeared as if a peculiar spell had come over a great many members of that General Conference who knew nothing of the decision of the Committee. The report was as follows:

"We have had before us certain papers asking the election of a man of African descent to our episcopal office, and other papers asking that the residence of such bishop be in Liberia. It is claimed in these petitions that the circumstances of the people of African descent are such that the efficiency of the work of our Church among them demands the election of a man of African descent to our episcopacy; that such election, more than any other fact, would establish beyond all gainsaying the relation of our Church to its members of African descent; that it would give them a bishop that could mingle freely with them without embarrassment to the work among them in any locality; that these ends would be reached, and the needed administration in Liberia be secured, by fixing the residence of such bishop in that colony. Your committee have considered these facts; but in view of the statement received from the present Board of Bishops as to their ability to discharge the duties of the superintendency, we recommend the adoption of the following:

"*Resolved*, (1) That this General Conference elect no bishops.

"*Resolved*, (2) That the facts presented in the several petitions above mentioned are entitled to careful consideration whenever the election of additional bishops shall become necessary.

"*Resolved*, (3) That we reiterate the declaration of the General Conference of 1872, touching the relation of a man of African descent to our episcopal office, and assert that race, nationality, color, or previous condition is no bar to the election of any man to the episcopal office in our Church, nor any other elective office filled by the General Conference."   (Journal 1876, p. 353.)

The fact that "papers asking that the residence of such bishop be in Liberia" had also been presented, though coming in all probability from opposition to the election of a man of African descent to the bishopric, like Thomas doubting his risen Lord, demonstrates the fact that that General Conference, by its Committee on Episcopacy, would have granted the petitioners in favor of the election to the episcopacy of a man of African descent their request, if they had produced a suitable man of African descent; or that the election of a missionary bishop for Liberia would put a quietus upon the agitation. If not this, then it declares that there were those in that General Conference who had expressed themselves as favoring every move touching the colored membership in the Church that would elevate and inspire them with hope for the future. The entire proceeding is, to my mind, inexplicable, were it not for the omnipresent fact that, so far as the Church is concerned, "God is in the midst of her."   The plea of the petitioners was not granted by that General Conference; but that is not stranger than the fact that other plans failed to be carried out at that General Conference, and for that matter every General Conference in the history of the Church from 1844 until to-day, that were, so far as arrangements, etc., go, already well supported before the meeting of the General Conference. Going back to the day of the adjournment of *that* General Conference, we say, we can wait.

THE GENERAL CONFERENCE OF 1880.—During the following quadrennium up to this General Conference the colored bishop question was more generally discussed than before. The official papers of the Church began to take notice of the question, while our brethren of the African and Methodist Episcopal Church, South, joined in to help on the good work—the former, in all probability, because of the supposed predicament it put the colored members into; and the latter, because they wished to push what they were pleased to call "the thorn in the flesh" farther into the quick of the white membership in the Church. The Baltimore District of the Washington Annual Conference passed a series of resolutions touching this question. Those resolutions were, in all probability, too radical when they declared the election of a man of African descent to our episcopacy "the only way the Church can hope to prove its good faith or respect for the numerous colored membership within the Church." The fact is, the Church was not required to bring forth fruits to exhibit any such thing.

The *Central Christian Advocate,* our official organ at St. Louis, thus spoke on this subject:

"A few weeks ago the members of the Baltimore District Conference, Washington Annual Conference, passed a preamble and resolutions, in which they declare that members of African descent in the Methodist Episcopal Church do not enjoy practically the fullest recognition of Church fellowship and communion; that the only way to prove to them and the world that they are recognized as equals in the Church is the election of a man of African descent to the office of bishop; and they recommend their brethren to 'agitate' the question and, if necessary, to 'demand' the election of a colored bishop at the General Conference to be held in May, 1880. This is the action of a single district conference; to what extent it represents the opinions of the colored ministers of the Church we have no means of knowing; for, so far as we have observed, no other district conference has yet taken action on the subject.

"The action of a single district conference, however influential and worthy of consideration, scarcely brings a question before the Church sufficiently to make it at once a subject for general discussion in the official papers. We proposed, therefore, to wait and see whether the Baltimore District Conference represented the convictions of others than itself. But our editorial brethren of the Methodist Episcopal Church, South, caught it up at once as a choice morsel, which afforded them a nice opportunity to worry, as they believe, the white membership of our Church, and to sow dissension among the colored members. The Richmond *Advocate* declared that intense mortification and confusion would seize upon the whites when this action of their colored brethren became known, and that not an official paper of the Church would dare mention what had taken place. It was a false prophet. And it must have been doubly surprised when the New York *Methodist*, which is presumed to represent the more conservative element in the Methodist Episcopal Church, promptly pronounced in favor of the election of one or two colored bishops. The Louisville *Methodist* thinks we have 'a difficult problem' on our hands, and, with an air of compassionate concern, informs our colored brethren 'that all the important offices of the Methodist Episcopal Church will be filled by white men, notwithstanding the resolutions of the Baltimore District.'

"But the Louisville *Methodist* is too anxious to make out a case. It says that the colored members of our Church were greatly disappointed that a colored bishop was not elected in 1872. Had the editor consulted the published proceedings of that General Conference instead of drawing upon his imagination for his facts, he would have scarcely made such a statement. There was but one memorial before the conference on the subject, and it had only four signatures attached. The Committee on

Episcopacy, to which it was referred, reported 'that, in their judgment, there is nothing in race, color, or former condition that is a bar to an election to the episcopacy, the true course being for us to elect only such persons as are, by their pre-eminent piety, endowments, culture, general fitness, and ac-. ceptability, best qualified to fill the office.' And no more eloquent speech was made during the conference than that of Hon. James Lynch, of Mississippi, a colored lay member, declaring that the colored men asked no favors on account of race, and that when they ˙produced a man as fit for the place as those about them, it would then be time enough for action."

The spirit manifested by our Southern brethren in the discussion of this question within our Church smacks of officiousness. They are in no way to be affected whether it is or is not done. While they have a perfect right to take part in any and all discussions worthy of public attention, anything like an attempt to sow the seeds of dissension among the members of any other denomination is, in the eyes of an ignorant black man, reprehensible, not to say unchristian. It gives room for complaint from the world that Southern "Methodists are no better than other folks." The colored man who is simply a member of the Methodist Episcopal Church for the sake of "important offices" had better *leave it—the sooner the better.* No Christian white man remains in any Church for that sole reason; and, as Bishop Simpson once said: "A white man is as good as a colored man, if he behaves himself." One thing is certain, that every such office-seeking colored man in the Church will fail to receive the support of every intelligent colored Christian within the Church. It is true that, on general principles, it was but a short time until the desire of the brethren of the Baltimore District became that of many others; that is, that it was thought necessary that a colored man should be elected to the bishopric.

When the General Conference of 1880 met in Cincinnati for its twenty-third session, this question again came up for discussion. Memorials and resolutions on this subject were presented from Washington Conference, by Henry A. Carroll; from Delaware Conference, by W. F. Butler, Zoar Church and Cambridge charge; J. C. Hartzell, from New Orleans preachers' meeting; by John H. Dunn and J. H. Shumpert, from Mississippi, *et al.;* and C. O. Fisher presented an extract from the journal of Savannah Conference and from Atlanta District. On Wednesday, May 12th, on motion, the rules were suspended to allow E. W. S. Hammond to present the following paper:

"WHEREAS, It is clearly evident, from the memorials and petitions on the subject, and which were duly referred to the Committee on Episcopacy, that the colored people of the Methodist Episcopal Church desire a bishop of their own race; and *whereas,* the election of a colored bishop would be a practical recognition of our full manhood by the Church, and a grand influence in the extension of our work in the United States and in other lands; and *whereas,* the General Conference of 1872 did declare, and the General Conference of 1876 did reaffirm, with emphatic significance, that race, nationality, color, or previous condition is no bar to the election of any man to the episcopal office in our Church; and *whereas,* the General Conference of 1876 did recommend that the memorials, petitions, etc., on the above-named subject should be entitled to a careful consideration whenever the election of additional bishops shall become necessary; and *whereas,* the necessity for the election of additional bishops is apparent, and the way is now open for the practical operation of the above resolution; be it, therefore,

"*Resolved,* That this General Conference recommend the election of a colored man to the episcopacy."

He supported the above preamble and resolution by a vigorous and timely speech, through courtesy of the General Conference, lasting over fifteen minutes.

On motion of L. C. Queal, the foregoing paper was laid on the table *for the present.* The memorials, followed hard by that resolution and speech, seemed to put the General Conference to thinking on the subject as never before.

It is not exactly certain that there was *no* opposition to the question at that General Conference.

Why need any one demand a thing to which there is no objection? It would come as a matter of course. Some spirit of opposition anon manifested itself in a way as unfair as uncalled for. For instance, the following presented by A. W. Milby, of Wilmington Conference:

"Whereas, The question of a colored bishop is with great persistency urged upon the attention of the General Conference; and *whereas*, it is a question to be determined, not by appeals to sentiment, but by arguments and facts addressed to the reason and the understanding; and *whereas*, we believe that the records of the benevolent societies and the statistical reports of the several annual conferences, composed of colored preachers, will furnish the best data for a wise and godly judgment; therefore,

"*Resolved*, That the Committee on Episcopacy be, and are hereby, instructed to inquire into and report to this conference at an early day, the following items in respect to the conferences composed, in whole or in part, of colored preachers, to wit: (1) The amount of money contributed by said conferences to the Episcopal Fund during the last quadrennium. (2) The amount contributed to the missionary cause. (3) The amount contributed to the Church Extension Society. (4) The amount contributed to the Freedmen's Aid Society. (5) The amount received by said conferences from the Missionary Society during the quadrennium. (6) The amount received from the Church Extension Society. (7) The amount received from the Freedmen's Aid Society."

On motion, the above resolutions were referred to the Committee on Episcopacy. The unfairness of such a proposition, as well as the unchristian spirit that produced it, become at once apparent, when it is remembered that in the Church of God the good to be done for our brother is not to depend either upon his willingly accepting it, demonstration of appreciation, the amount of wealth possessed by the recipients, or the amount of money they can or will produce. "How much will he bring at auction?" was the language of slave-traders in the past. The amount given for almost any cause by almost every person is dependent upon the intelligence possessed or communicated relating thereto, and the interest taken therein, coupled, of course, with financial ability. If the resolutions above referred to were germane, why not have each of the above conferences also report: (1) How many souls have been converted during the quadrennium? (2) How much religious fervor, comparative consistency in religious life, has been manifest among them? (3) How much time have they had, and under what circumstances, to be prepared to accumulate wealth, and then give it "as the Lord prospers them?" (4) What have they given, *per capita*, in comparison with their white brethren's wealth, time, and influence, for the spread of the kingdom of God among men ? (5) What proportion do they sustain to the rest of the membership of the Methodist Episcopal Church, numerically? (6) What per cent of their actual wealth do they give for the cause of Christ? If any special attention was paid to those resolutions, those in charge of our benevolent societies have no knowledge of it. The *Church of God will never require such a test.* Were the Methodist Church to do it, Satan would certainly be warranted in affirming that a dollar in her scales weighs more than an immortal soul.

The crisis in the question of a colored bishop came May 20th, when Report No. 3 of the Committee on Episcopacy was presented, as follows:

"The Committee on Episcopacy, having considered the memorials and petitions referred to it on the election of a bishop of African descent, adopted each of the following resolutions by a vote of thirty-nine to eight:

"*Resolved*, 1. That the best interests of our Church in general, and of our colored people in particular, require that one or more of our general superintendents should be of African descent.

" *Resolved*, 2. That we recommend that this General Conference elect one bishop of African descent."

J. S. Smart moved to adopt; thereupon Alfred Wheeler presented the following minority report, and moved that it be substituted for the report of the majority:

"A portion of your Committee on Episcopacy,

differing widely from the majority, both as to the necessity and expediency of electing a colored bishop at the present time, feel constrained to express our dissent by a minority report. After listening attentively to prolonged discussions upon the subject, and giving due weight to the arguments urged in its favor, and to full representation of the state of our religious work among the colored people of the South, representations made by themselves as well as by their white co-laborers, we are convinced that sound policy forbids the adoption of the recommendation of the majority.

" *Resolved*, therefore, That we deem it inexpedient to elect any more bishops at this General Conference."

John Lanahan moved that the whole subject be indefinitely postponed. On motion of Emperor Williams, the yeas and nays were called, and the motion to postpone indefinitely was carried by two hundred and twenty-eight votes to one hundred and thirty-seven.

To show the interest manifested, of the three hundred and ninety-nine delegates, all were present and voted on that resolution save thirty-four. At page 282 of General Conference Journal of 1880 we have the list of names. There appear names of persons who voted indefinitely to postpone that question that surprises us a little; and not very much, either. However, a quietus was thus put upon that question for *that session at least.*

Let us look back for a moment. Has it not appeared in nearly every instance, when the colored membership have memorialized the General Conference, that not only has respectful attention been given, but concessions made? Has it not appeared as clearly, all the way through, that the Church, as such, is ready whenever the race presents a proper man? The voice of the Church not only declares its willingness, but even hints that while " race, color," nor other special considerations are to be helps or hindrances, *it is possible* to elect a colored bishop by " fair and honorable competition between the friends of the respective candidates."

There is no man within the Methodist Episcopal Church who would feel worse than the writer, were any General Conference of our Church to elect a white man to the episcopacy because he had been an Abolitionist, a Federal soldier, was a Japanese, or who had been a foreign missionary, but, aside from these things, had no other qualification. Just the same way would it be if any General Conference should elect to the office of bishop in our Church a *colored* man, simply because he had been a slave, or because he could make a passable speech, or deliver an acceptable sermon, or was pastor of a small congregation, but, aside from this, had no literary attainments, but little or no executive ability, and but little practical experience in general Church work. It would be no particular advantage under such circumstances, while it might do incalculable injury, not only to the general Church, but to the interests of the race in particular.

Hon. James Lynch, of Mississippi, declared in the General Conference of 1872, that no favors were asked on account of race. Rev. E. W. S. Hammond, in the eloquent speech delivered before the General Conference of 1880, in Cincinnati, said that the plea being made was not for a *colored bishop simply for the colored people*, but a bishop for the Methodist Episcopal Church. And now the way is not only open, but wisdom at the threshold of the bishopric in our Church cries to all, "There is nothing in race, color, or previous condition, a bar to entrance here, but the true course given me is to admit only those who, by their pre-eminent piety, godly judgment, and literary qualifications, are best fitted to fill the office." There is not an intelligent Christian of color within our Church that does not bow assent to this sentiment. When as a race we are to be represented on our bench of bishops, we want a man who is, and will be, a credit to the Church, an honor to the race and to himself, an equal among equals in every respect—a representative man, "blameless, the husband of one wife, vigilant, sober, modest, given to hospitality, apt to teach; not given to wine, no striker, not greedy of filthy lucre; but patient, not a brawler, not covetous; one that ruleth well his own household; not a novice, lest being lifted up with pride he fall into the condemnation of the devil. Moreover he must

have a good report of them which are without, lest
he fall into reproach and the snare of the devil."
Then, and not till then, ought a colored man be
elected as " one of the bishops of the Methodist
Episcopal Church."

CHAPTER X.

WHY ASK FOR A BISHOP OF AFRICAN DESCENT?

DO not the attitude sustained by the colored man to the Church, from his admission into the John Street Church in New York, and the actions taken by the Church relating to his interests, based as they have been upon the integrity and fidelity of the race, up to the granting of separate Conferences, warrant it? If not, why were not our German brethren satisfied until they were represented nationally or linguistically therein? The Church has hitherto carried out the most natural, as well as rational order of succession in this matter, that, if it leads anywhere, leads up, *necessarily* leads up, to *this point.* The colored ministers were recognized, licensed, given appointments, quarterly conferences, district and annual conferences, the presiding eldership, admitted as delegates to the General Conferences, elected to General Conference offices, and the Church declared that " race, color, or previous condition " was " no bar to election to the episcopacy in our Church." If we are required and expected to go on to perfection, will any one deny that election to the episcopacy will push the whole race a step higher in the Divine life? Not simply because of this alone, but because the colored

Rev. A. E. P. ALBERT, D. D.,
Editor of Southwestern Christian Advocate,
NEW ORLEANS, LA.

man, like white men, believes the bishopric a step higher, in office at least, than the eldership in our Church. He believes, like other men, that progression is the watchword of the hour. Who does not now know that a bishop in the Methodist Episcopal Church is considered the most influential minister in the State, county, city, village, and in the general Church? No other office is paramount. The fact that there is to be allowed *no discrimination* on account of race, color, or previous condition of servitude within the Church, it is claimed, guarantees to them not only the right to ask, but to *expect* help in securing the same, since it will never be possible for it to be done by the race alone within the Church.

It is therefore declared by many of both races within the Church, that *justice to the race demands it as it could not for any other class of members within the Church.* Nothing less than injustice can withhold that which is justly due. Now the colored members, whose influence has brought them forth into prominence in the Church, have never asked the General Conference to elect a bishop of African descent because our bishops have been one thing to white members and another to colored members, nor because our bishops, when coming among the colored members, have been "overseers" instead of superintendents, nor because they are not acceptable to the colored membership. Far from it. Our bishops to-day hold a place in the hearts of the colored membership of the Church that any man of

African descent, elected to the episcopacy in our Church, could only desire, since he could not dislodge his white colleague. But it is asked for the same reason the Church gave years ago for the proper recognition of colored ministers when it said, it is "a principle patent to Christian enterprise that the missionary field itself must produce the most efficient missionaries." Is not this an argument at once logically true in the case of a bishop of African descent? The reasons given by representatives from the South when asking for a separate conference were: (1) "It will secure greater efficiency in the prosecution of the work, since many things of great interest to an annual conference and to the Church never get farther than the humblest hearthstone." (2) "It will relieve us from the taunts and sneers of designing men," and secure the communion and friendship of many who would not otherwise unite with us. (3) "It will relieve the Church of even a suspicion of a spirit of caste, and make us feel as men, and the peers of our white brethren. (4) It will be no innovation upon any principle of Christianity or of our beloved Church," but will mightily help in "rending the veil" and breaking down the middle wall of partition Satan has built between brethren out of the remains of slavery that existed in this country. Another reason is offered on the score of the numerical standing of the colored membership.

According to the statistics of 1884, there are

now not far from 1,800,000 members within the Church. Of this number, there are about 300,000 colored members. "The constitutional rights of the colored members" being recognized, indeed all their rights and privileges, it would follow that, on general principles, one member in the Church has as many and varied rights as another. The colored members in the Church make up one-sixth of its membership. They would on this scale, therefore, be entitled to one representative on our bench of bishops for every six, and so on.

Will the time ever come when a colored bishop will be elected by the General Conference of the Methodist Episcopal Church? This the future will tell. However ignorant we may now be as to whether it will ever be done or not, we can easily imagine the result of such an election. It would no doubt be as the bursting forth of some pent-up fountain which sends forth streams in opposite directions. Doubtless if there remain any within the Church who fear man more than God, they would likely flow outward toward more congenial climes, where the nursing of wrath brings imaginary peace. It is impossible to turn a mighty stream all at once out of its channel without some commotion. But then. the onsweeping tide would soon wear another channel, and no more would be seen of the commotion than anon a ripple in the mighty stream. The other stream, flowing in the opposite direction, would be, to the Christian men and women of this land, "a stream that makes glad the city of God." It would send a thrill of renewed vigor and confidence in God and Methodism all over this world. Every community where infidelity, skepticism, or Romanism now predominates would be hopelessly stunned, while a gainsaying world would not only stand aghast, but fall back before the enthusiastic shout of seven million hitherto rejected and ostracized images of God cut in ebony. It would be an incentive to Christians everywhere in general, and the three hundred thousand colored members, old and young, within the Church in particular, to live better lives and do better work. The older men who now hold positions of prominence in the Church would have more time in which to do their work, and would probably do it better, at any rate more hopefully. Instead of having to fight caste prejudice, and repel the insults heaped upon them hitherto by that hateful spirit, they would quietly prosecute their work. The younger men, who are already within the colored conferences would feel a desire, even if they were unable to make amends for lost time, better to prepare themselves for future usefulness. The colored annual conferences would at once begin to fasten the breaches in their fences, through which candidates for clerical orders have been creeping at times. The young men who would come flocking to the doors of the conferences for admission would find written over the archway, "No *young* man admitted to this conference until he shall be found possessed with the necessary qualifications,—'gifts, grace, and usefulness.'"

Our college alumni, who have gone elsewhere seeking employment, would return. How much more proficient does that man try to be who knows there is a future before him, than the one who suspects there is none! Thousands of our talented young people have left us because they said they saw but little hope in the future for the colored ministry in our Church. Indeed, there was a time in the history of our colored work when the professional man, the mechanic, and the man of means among us, were all about to leave us in some localities, because it had been told them that within the Church we were but "hewers of wood and drawers of water."

There was also a time when graduates of our institutions, in many instances, were given work by other denominations because we had none for them before they took their diploma from the campus of their *alma mater*. Why, it is impossible properly to educate a man, and then keep him from thinking, looking, and speaking for himself. It is only recently that the younger people of the race have become interested in our work. This is directly attributable to our separate conferences; while many who left us for "sufficient reasons" would return, and we could more securely hold those we now have.

THE SEGREGATION OF THE RACE INTO COLORED ORGANIZATIONS.

It is impossible to build up a first-class member-ship out of second-class material. This has been one of our weak points. Such efforts as "Tanner's Apology" were aimed along this line. Now, why is it that in New York, Pennsylvania, New Jersey, and, for that matter, everywhere in this country except in the Southern States, the colored man has sought a colored organization? Why the segregation of the race in the North, where slavery never came? Dr. A. G. Haygood believes, with many others, that race instinct segregates them. He says: "Instinct never yet surrendered to arguments; it is their race instinct, deep and strong and inexpugnable," as Carlyle would say. Who that heard their impas-sioned speeches at Cincinnati, in May, 1880, could not see that their appeal came, not from the cold conclusions of the reason, but red-hot out of their hearts, from the irresistible promptings of instinct? Listening to their speeches, I felt strongly the mighty under-current that their words but feebly revealed, and I felt—"They are right; they do well to ask this conference for a bishop of their own race." Listening to the words of the white leaders of the conference, and looking at the subject in the light of cold judgment, I said to myself: "This conference is also right to decline the request." This instinctive disposition to form Church affilia-tions on the color basis may be wise or unwise.

But it is in them—deep in them. The tendency is strengthening all the time. This instinct will never rest satisfied till it realizes itself in complete separations. The movements that grow out of race instincts do not wait upon the conclusions of philosophy; nor do they, for a long time, take counsel of policy. We may, all of us, as well adjust our plans to the determined and inevitable movements of this instinct, that does not reason, but that moves steadily and resistlessly to accomplish its ends. It is a very grave question to be considered by all who have responsibility in the matter, whether over-repression of race instincts may not mar their normal evolution; may not introduce elements unfriendly to healthful growth; may not result in explosions. I have seen a heavy stone wall overturned by a root that was once a tiny white fiber. Instinct is like the life-force that expresses itself in life or death.

Let us see. "Is it race instinct" that tends to segregate the colored man? We answer, No. His desire to segregate is only a self-defensive measure. The colored man in this country is *desperately* in earnest in his effort to remove every vestige of the prejudice against him arising from his previous condition of·servitude. In the North he found that the white people knew him only as a slave or a freedman. If the former, then he was considered a mendicant—ignorant, superstitious, and immoral, as a natural result of slavery. They could not think of taking him into their homes—

cultured, refined, and religious homes—to be at once associated with the members of their families. As to their Churches, he was wholly unfitted for their mode of worship; for to him it appeared foolishness, fashion, and fastidiousness, void of "the true, heart-felt religion" of the plantation where "his sons and his daughters prophesied, his old men dreamed dreams, and his young men saw visions." As a result, he pretty soon began to feel uneasy, and sighed for "the seasons of the past." The white man of the North *could not possibly meet the social or religious demands of the slave.* If he put him in the parlor or school-room with white children, or in the congregation of the Lord—though given a front seat, and in every conceivable way made welcome—he was uneasy. Rev. Richard Allen says that it "was quite a task for me to preach the gospel in St. George's Church, in Philadelphia." The white man of the North could not make the colored man from the South feel at home. If he had had a separate building in which to allow him and his family to live, it would have appeared more like home to him. I do not here speak of the many noble exceptions, for we all know "what's bred in the bone is not easily eradicated from the flesh." It is a hard matter, indeed, in after years to change all at once the habits of men's past lives, whether they be religious, moral, or temporal. Again, the white man of the North had no work the colored man of the South was adapted to do. The house-work usually was done either by "the hale housewife with busy care," or by a foreign domestic. The same was true of the out-door work. All this in the South the colored man enjoyed without a rival. The whole affair was in an abnormal condition with the colored man from the South. Those who doubt these statements have but to note the line of demarkation that is not even yet effaced between the "free colored man of the North" and the former slave colored man of the South, to-day, everywhere. Their mode of Church polity, songs, prayers, sermons, dress, deport-ment, and all, are different. This to-day makes—for awhile at least—the colored man of the South in the North shy, not to say uncomfortable. What relation could be farther from the wishes of the poor, ignorant, and superstitious colored man of those days than the social equality granted him? What could make him wish more to be carried "back to his old Kentucky home?"

Every effort or advance made by the white man toward the colored man found his superstition of white men repulsive. First, the thought would come to him, "I should suspect some danger nigh, where I possess delight." Again, the colored man of the South knew nothing of business principles in general, and of the *Yankee* idea of business princi-ples in particular. When the rigid rules of active business life were exacted of him by his white Northern neighbor or employer, it was but a sad

contrast to the loose and illegitimate business principles he had been under in the South, and it was
but a short time until he naturally began to suspect
that the Northern white man thought he was a
thief. Again, after the war the better class of colored men—such as the land-owner, the stock-raiser,
the mechanic, and the farmer, and those who had
some learning—did not go North. In 1870 there
were residing in sixteen Southern States, beginning
with Missouri, west with Texas, and east with the
Carolinas, 4,609,541, being 15.8 of the whole population; leaving but 726,521 colored people elsewhere in these United States. As late as 1880
there were 6,200,646 colored people in the United
States, while there were but 180,393 residing in
Northern States. It took but very little inducement to make the colored man believe, therefore,
that while the white man of the North had helped to
free him, he now cared but little for him. It is
true that "birds of a feather do flock together,"
especially young birds; at any rate, throughout the
animal, vegetable, and mineral kingdoms the exam-
ple is given by nature to man, in that all these only
flourish *in congenial climates and soil,* while for
all his life the colored man had been taught to suspect the Yankee as only loving him for what he
could get out of him. Again, in the South the colored man had seen and become conversant with the
irresponsible, careless plantation life, and with the
prodigality of his master, who thought nothing of

tossing him a quarter now and then. Up North the last farthing was exacted from him; he was expected to pay his house-rent, grocery bill, keep clean, and make but little noise around his home, at Church, and on the public thoroughfares. This to him—recently liberated—was all new and strange. If he became disorderly, the white man of the North, instead of laughing at him, and passing on the other side, would at once have him arrested; if dishonest, punished. He had been used to "better things," as he thought; and hence it took but little persuasion for him to believe the white man of the North not as friendly as the Southern white man.

To say that the cultivation of such superstition on the part of some of the so-called leading colored men was an advantage; that such talk from the "book-learned colored man," who either *thought* he spoke the truth or perjured himself, had the effect of segregating the colored people into separate Churches, is apparent to all. The statement of the colored man who is reported to have established a bank for colored folks is, to my mind, illustrative at this point. When he had accumulated two or three thousand dollars of the money of his people he tacked a card on his front door with this inscription: "This bank am busted." When his depositors came in great crowds about his door, and loudly called for him, he came forth and said: " Now, gentlemuns and ladies, we is free. We must act jus' like white folks do. White folks put money in der banks and de banks burst; and when dey see it, den dat's de end ob de matter. So it mus' be wid us." This is said to have satisfied the creditors.

When some colored men saw the advantage of segregating the colored people, they found a great amount of *gratuitous help*. Every white man, woman, and child, who objected to " Negro equality," at once lent his or her aid. The white orator and editor and preacher of this class joined with the so-called leader in segregating the colored people. *This no sane man will deny.* And now, in these latter days, philosophers arise and declare it "instinct." Everything was in favor of the segregation. A great many white men, as well as a great many good colored men, deprecated this, and fought desperately against it. In " Chauncey Judd " we have an illustration of this spirit, even as early as Colonial days. A Presbyterian minister was invited to marry a free colored couple. The bargain the groom made with the clergyman was, that if he would marry him like a white man he would pay him like a white man. The bride was very pretty, but as large and black as pretty. The guests were of both races. It was customary at that day for the clergyman to kiss the bride. This the clergyman forgot to do, for some reason. When about to take leave of the couple the clergyman incidentally remarked that the ceremony was incomplete without "the fee." "Why," said the groom, "I sticks to de contrac'." "Well, that is right," said the clergyman, "for you said if I would marry you like a white man you would pay me like a white man." "That's jus' so," said the groom, "but you did n't kiss the bride." "O well," said the clergyman, "that is no matter, any way." "O well, it's no matter 'bout de fee, any way," said the groom.

Colored men who aspired to leadership among the colored people, and were willing to stoop so low, when they knew better, saw that the support of colored men, politically, religiously, or morally, would at once bring them prestige, influence, and power with white men. To segregate the colored people would, as Rev. Richard Allen intimated, create "a necessity" for his services. If they remained associated with white people, there would soon come a time when it would be impossible for him to be of service to his people so as to benefit himself pecuniarily. We do not aim here to charge all leaders of the race, political or ecclesiastical, with perfidy, but to prove that it is not "instinct" alone that is responsible for the segregation of the race, or that this instinct will not allow them to associate on perfect equality with white people; that it is not ordained of God that colored members must be under colored pastors in colored Churches, controlled by colored men *exclusively.* That the disposition of the more intelligent colored man of the North rather seeks separation or independency, than segregation, is being ocularly demonstrated annually, and becoming more acceptable as he becomes more cultured. If this be not so, why is it that the cultured young colored man, who "tips" his education in some Eastern or Northern college, comes back South, dissatisfied to remain? Dr. Haygood must find some better and more philosophical answer.

It is a fact that a great many colored men who aspire to leadership politically and ecclesiastically, will deny what we have here said. Indeed, we would have hesitated to speak so plainly were it not that we wish, as much as possible, to give the bare facts of the case as they appear to us, aside from any personal consideration. We believe, with all the earnestness and candor of soul and mind, that this whole "color-line" question, from beginning to end, lies at the feet of those aspirants; that most of the opprobium, ostracism, and caste prejudice that did and do now exist against the race in this country, can be, and is, impartially and legitimately traced to that source; and that the separate African Churches in this country are the parents of not less than ninety-five per cent of this hue and cry against Negro social equality. They are easily conceived, therefore, to be the causes of all other ecclesiastical unrest and "color-line" separations in this country. This is so evident that he who runs may read it.

CHAPTER XI.

THE GENERAL CONFERENCE OF 1884.

TO the General Conference of 1880 there was presented a memorial from " the leading educators (fifty in number) in our white schools in the South," asking that the work of the Freedmen's Aid Society be extended so as to aid the schools of the Church in the South where only white pupils attended. No special emphasis was put upon the matter, save that of "aiding" the above-named schools. The Committee on Freedmen's Aid Work in the South carefully considered the subject, and reported to that conference as follows:

"Your Committee on Freedmen's Aid and Southern Work respectfully report:

"1. That, in its judgment, the present organization of the Freedmen's Aid Society should remain unchanged.

"2. That under the phrase 'and others' of Article II, in the Constitution of the Freedmen's Aid Society, we see the way clear to aid the schools which have been established by our Church in the Southern States among the white people, and hereby ask the General Conference to recommend to the Board of Managers of this society to give such aid to these schools during the next quadrennium as can be done without embarrassment to the schools among the freedmen."

As soon as the report was read, considerable feeling was apparent. The question had hitherto seemed of small importance. While the report was pending the feeling manifest found vent in "a motion to appropriate twenty-five per cent of all moneys raised by the Freedmen's Aid Society to schools among the whites." It was laid on the table. After this there seemed a determination to separate, if possible, the educational work of the Church in the South among the whites from that of the blacks. Rev. A. J. Kynett, therefore, offered the following as a substitute for the second item :

"*Resolved,* That the Board of Education be, and is hereby, instructed to make such provisions as may be necessary and practicable for the aid of our educational institutions in the South not aided by the Freedmen's Aid Society."

Had this substitute been accepted, we certainly would have had two separate and distinct educational societies within the Church; the Educational Society would have been so burdened as to have had to withdraw, to a certain extent, from the plan of aiding indigent students as hitherto, or increase its resources. That, at any rate, to have thus burdened it would have crippled, if not killed it, is suspected. That substitute was covered by the following as a substitute for the whole:

Resolved, That in the judgment of this General

Conference the present organization and perpetuity of the Freedmen's Aid Society should remain unchanged."

But both these substitutes were laid on the table. The other extreme view was manifested by the following substitute, which went the way of the preceding:

"*Resolved*, 1. That the collections of the Freedmen's Aid Society shall be wholly appropriatde to aid the schools for the colored people.

"*Resolved*, 2. That the Committee on Education be requested to make provisions for giving aid to schools among the white people of the South."

That a disposition to separate the educational work of the Church in the South between the races prevailed, appears on the face of the foregoing. The report, as given above, was then adopted. It is plainly seen that the Church did not, even in this, intend to be partial on account of race or color. One would naturally infer from the foregoing and that which follows, that considerable feeling was manifested. In Report No. 2 of the Committee on Freedmen appears the following:

"*Resolved*, That our pastors, in presenting the claims of this society to the Church, should remind our people that a portion of the appropriations of the society will be made for the education of the white population connected with our Church in the Southern States, but not to the embarrassment of the work among our people of color."

This, in itself, showed that the friends to the educational work of the Church among the white people of the South were on the alert; that the next General Conference would have to speak out as to aiding them.

During the quadrennium following the adjournment of that General Conference the question of changing the name of the Freedmen's Aid Society was discussed. During the discussion it was very evident that "the color-line" was being crossed and recrossed, denied and affirmed, objected to and supported, execrated and declared a blessing. Some declared that the reason for wanting the name of the society changed was: (1) Not simply that the society might help more largely in carrying on educational work begun by our white membership in the South, but (2) to make them eligible to such aid without being considered second to the colored man, or seeming to have to accept the crumbs that fall from the colored man's table, prepared for him by the Methodist Episcopal Church in the presence of his enemies; (3) that those who are willing to aid in the educational work of the Church among the whites, without *any* of it being used to help colored students, may have a chance thus to display their liberality; (4) that those within the Church who have all along refused to contribute to the support of the benevolences of the Church because of their objection to the bringing in of this Gentile proselyte on an equal footing, may have a chance to empty their liberal gifts into the coffers of the Church. Indeed, so high ran this discussion during the quadrennium, that some even went so far as to declare it an effort to fan anew the slumbering but not quenched embers of caste prejudice; to keep verdant the rank weeds of race prejudice that continue to grow rank and prolific in the swamps and bayous, on the mountains and hill-sides, the plains and valleys of some of our Church-work in the South. This question, in many minds, swung around to the previous conditions of the two races within the Church in the South. To give some idea of the previous conditions of the two races within the Church in the South hitherto, we quote from the address of the president of the society, Bishop Walden, the following:

"Our Church had access to two classes on entering this field,—the whites in North Carolina, Tennessee, Georgia, Alabama, Arkansas, and Texas, and the colored people in all of the States from which she had been excluded. The condition of these classes was different. The whites were impoverished by the war, but they had some possessions and some kinds of business; they had church-buildings, however dilapidated; but in some places all Church organizations had been disbanded, and in other places the connectional bonds were broken; they were ready, however, for reorganization, and in Eastern Tennessee almost an entire conference (the Holston) voluntarily sought and was given a place among our annual conferences. The colored people had not lost property, for they had none to lose; they had no Church organizations nor buildings, and their Church membership, at best, was only nominal; all they had was their recently proclaimed freedom and their hands trained to toil.

"Picture to yourselves for the moment those to whom our Church found an open door—the impoverished and almost churchless white people, and the colored people, who were not only without homes, but without the relations of the home; not only without earthly possessions, but impoverished in the best elements of their nature. It may be no marvel that societies were soon gathered and conferences soon organized among the whites, for with them it was chiefly a work of reorganization and edification. But what of the work among the freed people—those who had only toiled as house-servants and slave-mechanics and field-hands? Here, among them, the very foundations of Church-work had to be laid, and our first movement in this direction—the necessary and the right movement—was to give them, at once, their normal relation in and to the Church."

Let us examine the status of these two classes. The whites had been (1) "impoverished by the war," whether they took sides with the Union or against it. If the latter was the case, it is evident that they had been slaveholders themselves or friendly to the slave oligarchy. And yet these same people had left them some "possessions and some kinds of business." They had "church-buildings, however dilapidated. They were ready for reorganization." It was not so with the colored people. "These were without homes, without the relations of home; not only without earthly possessions, but impoverished in the best elements of their nature." These poor colored people had never had the advantages of any enlightening influences save such as came to "house-servants, slave-mechanics, and field-hands." How true is it that "here among them the very foundations of Church-work had to be laid." The Methodist Episcopal Church went down South hunting "the lost sheep of the house of Israel," for whom no denomination seemed to care much at that time. The whites had for twenty years, more or less, worshiped with, or were members of, the Southern Methodist Episcopal Church; a few standing alone and waiting till a better day appeared. Here was an opportunity also to turn aside and give aid to this other class of our membership in the South, by teaching them the doctrine of the Fatherhood of God and the brotherhood of man. Such men as Rev. John P. Newman and Bishop Gilbert Haven went down to help. Their eloquence, erudition, religious and moral force, told only here and there. Such men made but little headway toward the bringing in of "whole annual conferences" among the whites into our Church. They were unpopular save among the poor freedmen. Some of the white members of the Methodist Episcopal Church in the South have no interest in the work of the Methodist Episcopal Church that does not come to them unincumbered by any reminiscences of the past or present relations of the two races. The growth of our white membership in the South during the last ten years has been considerable. Is it not strange that the whites and the blacks within the Methodist Episcopal Church in the South sustain *to-day*, in some places, the same relation to each other that the Jews used to sustain to the Samaritans? Do we not find, just along here somewhere, the key to the situation in the South within our Church, as well as cause for the action of the General Conference above referred to?

If required to state from our own knowledge what is positively believed to be an ungarnished truth, we would say that so far as a majority of our white membership in the South is concerned we, as a Church, have not succeeded in dislodging a *single one* of the old prejudices against "race and color." It is known that there are beautiful exceptions, but they are like angels' visits to earth nowadays. The only redeeming feature has been, that the Church, as such, has never yielded a single point in favor of caste in the South. We have known instances where white preachers of white congregations in our Church in the South stayed away from colored annual conferences to keep from being introduced as members of our Church. The instances in the South in which the white ministers demanded a separate conference, because of the relations of the two races, are not few. The Methodist Episcopal Church understood all the while that this was the condition of affairs in every nine cases in ten in the South where "a color-line conference" was desired. Hence, the heart of the Church being right, she always put in "a proviso" when authorizing the creation or division of conferences.

The action taken by the General Conference of 1876 on the question, corroborates the above statement. It is as follows:

"The committee have, by a large sub-committee, given much time to its consideration, and have investigated carefully the matter referred to them. They have considered the numerous memorials, petitions, and resolutions presented to the General Conference on the subject, whether from annual conferences, conventions, or private individuals. They have consulted with most, if not all, the delegates to the General Conference, who represent conferences particularly interested in the question of division, and have studied the history of the movements in several conferences seeking to effect or prevent division within a few years past, and report the following result of its investigation."

Then follows a concise, yet full, statement of the reasons, pro and con, with this conclusion:

" From these facts, and after impartially inquiring

into the whole subject, your committee recommend for adoption the following resolutions:

" *Resolved*, 1. That where it is the general desire of the members of an annual conference that there should be no division of such conference into two or more conferences in the same territory; and where it is not clearly to be seen that such division would favor or improve the state of the work in any conference; and where the interests and usefulness of even a minority of the members of such conference, and of the members of Churches in such conference, might be damaged or imperiled by division, it is the opinion of this General Conference that such division should not be made.

" *Resolved*, 2. That whenever it shall be requested by a majority of the white members, and also a majority of the colored members, of any annual conference, that it be divided, then it is the opinion of this General Conference that such division should be made; and, in that case, the bishop presiding is hereby authorized to organize the new conference or conferences." (Journal, 1876, pp. 329–331.)

In the case of the division of the Tennessee Conference, the colored members retained the original name, and the whites had to find a descriptive, or rather distinctive, adjective to retain the "Tennessee" part of the name. In this case, if not in many others, general dissatisfaction and injury ensued. Aspiring colored men, in a number of our own colored conferences, allowed their aspirations for honors to exceed their better judgment, and hence voted "aye" when their hearts said "nay." There was, by the time the General Conference of 1884 met in Philadelphia, a party among the delegates who were determined to do one of two things; either to bring the white work within our Church (that was brought under the fostering care of the Freedmen's Aid Society by the words "and others" inserted in the constitution) up to an equal share of the money appropriated by the Church for its work in the South, or else have the Educational Society take *entire control* of the educational work among the whites. This would have shaded the demarkation caste-line to the satisfaction of his Satanic majesty, and at the same time turned into other channels the aid hitherto rendered by that society to indigent colored pupils, and would have, by this, made it popular indeed to be a white Methodist within the great Methodist Episcopal Church "without any unnecessary contamination with any disturbing element." The friends of humanity, equity, and righteousness also "trusted God, but kept their powder dry." The conference had but fairly got to work when the oncoming storm began to gather. J. M. Shumpert, under the call, presented the following, which was referred to the Committee on State of the Church:

"Inasmuch as there has been a great deal of discussion, both in the religious and secular press, of caste in the Methodist Episcopal Church; and inasmuch as caste is a curse to any nation, and more especially to a religious denomination; and inasmuch as we believe that caste prejudice is a sin, and is born of ignorance and hate, that it narrows the mind, embitters the heart, and harms the American citizens, both as men and as Christians; therefore, be it

"*Resolved*, That it is the sense of this General Conference that no trustees of churches, schools, colleges, or universities, nor any pastor, principal, president, or any other person in authority of church or school property, belonging to or under the control of the Methodist Episcopal Church, should exclude any person or persons from their churches, schools, colleges, or universities, of good moral character, on account of color, race, or previous condition of servitude."

This was the beginning of a conflict. At the General Conferences we all understand that the "fighting" is all done in the committee-room. That the spirit of this resolution was opposed in the committee-room no member of "the Committee on the State of the Church" will deny. To one who was at a great distance from the scene of action it appeared that the forty-three colored delegates in that General Conference could easily be seen to belong to the two elements that usually make up our General Conferences, the radical and conservative; but not equally divided. Indeed, there were not more than five "conservative" of the forty-three. Now I have used the words "radical" and "conservative," and mean by these terms just what they have meant in every General Conference of our Church since, if not before, 1840. The former believe in "hewing to the line, let the chips fall where they may." The other believes it better, for policy's sake, to be lenient to the extreme of compromise in some instances. In that General Conference the radicals desired to march into the field against caste prejudice, floating "the black flag." The conservatives wanted to be all things to some men that they might not lose any, and, at the same time, "save some." It is easy to see how the thirty-eight could go home and look their black constituents squarely in the face and say: "No timidity or other inducement persuaded me to depart from the wholesome teachings of common sense and race pride." Before the intended import of that last sentence is *misconstrued.* we add, the others, returning home, could easily have said to their constituents: "We have adopted a policy for future action that we hope will bring peace out of confusion." The ardent desire of the conservative faction to change the name of the Freedmen's Aid Society was closely connected, as all can easily see, with the question of caste prejudice—whether for or against we do not stop now to say. The question of mixed or separate schools among our members in the South had been discussed during the quadrennium.

The establishment of the Little Rock University—overshadowing that section of the country, as well as Philander Smith College, where colored youth were being educated—with that of the Chattanooga University, at Chattanooga, Tennessee, helped to agitate the question. It is said that the items touching this subject were presented in the General Conference by a resolution adopted without reference to a committee, through reports from the Committee on Freedmen's Aid and Work in the South, and through a resolution from the Committee on the State of the Church. Any criticism in opposition to work done for the whites by the Freedmen's Aid Society was broken by the General Conference adopting the following:

"*Resolved,* That we fully indorse the administration of the Freedmen's Aid Society during the past quadrennium."

This is the resolution above referred to. The following was part of the work done and reported to that General Conference as its administration during the quadrennium:

" The following sums were appropriated to schools among whites:

In 1879 and 1880, ...	. . .
In 1880 and 1881, ...	$2,600 00
In 1881 and 1882, ...	19,453 75
In 1882 and 1883, ...	26,847 25
Total receipts during quadrennium, ...	$437,986 89
Appropriations for schools among whites, . .	48,901 00
Appropriations for schools among colored, . .	$389,085 89

"The whites received a little less than one-ninth of the receipts, and a little less than one-eighth as much as the colored people."

It is to be remembered that "the schools among the whites" were not constitutionally eligible to aid from the Freedmen's Aid Society until after the General Conference of 1880; that the work had been chiefly confined to its then legitimate channel, the colored work, and, of course, appropriations to the work among the colored people began with the work of the society. Viewed from that point, another phase of appropriations appears.

Resolutions came rather briskly and presenting many different phases of the question. On May 12th, Rev. C. O. Fisher, of the Savannah Conference, presented the following resolution, signed by himself and twenty-two others, which, on motion, was adopted:

"*Resolved*, That the General Conference hereby confirms and reaffirms the opinion previously expressed that 'color is no bar to any right or privilege of office or membership in the Methodist Episcopal Church,' but we recognize the propriety of such administration as will hereafter, as heretofore, secure the largest concession to individual preferences on all questions involving merely the social relations of its members."

Now, the above resolution in some way or other, was afterward the cause of no little dispute as to who was the author of it, and who signed it.

There followed some discussion, through the papers, between Dr. Marshall W. Taylor and Dr. Fisher as to it. Like Topsy in Uncle Tom's Cabin, it seems to have had no parents at all, "but jus' growed up." *Its purport, some declare, was not indorsed by all who signed it.* It, however, was a tally for the conservative element, whether so intended or not.

Report No. 3 of Committee on Freedmen's Aid and Work in the South was adopted May 22d, as follows:

"Your Committee on Freedmen's Aid and Work in the South have carefully considered the several memorials referred to us, involving the question of separate or mixed schools for the accommodation of our colored and white membership in the South, and as the result of our deliberations present the following:

"It is an historical fact, highly honorable to the Methodist Episcopal Church, that she has been the constant friend of the common people, and especially of the colored man.

"The Freedmen's Aid Society, organized for the purpose of aiding in the education and elevation of the freedmen, is the unanswerable proof of our friendship to them in the hour of their need. Twenty-four institutions of learning—academies, seminaries, colleges, and theological schools—established and maintained among them at a cost of more than $1,250,000 for the benefit of the colored people, constitute a magnificent demonstration of our devotion, which requires no elaboration and admits of no denial.

"The management of this portion of our educational work, we believe, in the main, has been wise, efficient, and successful. Our effort in this direction should not be relaxed, but increased.

"The establishment of schools for the benefit of our white membership in the South we believe to have been a wise and necessary measure. Their success has been gratifying. The beneficial results have not been confined to those immediately interested, but their liberalizing effects upon public sentiment have greatly redounded to the advantage of our colored people. We regret that, for so great and important a work, so little has been done by the Church, and we desire most emphatically to give expression to our conviction that the time has come when this portion of our educational work should be strengthened and placed upon a strong and permanent basis, as its importance certainly demands. To the question of mixed schools we have given our most serious and prayerful attention. It is a subject beset with peculiar difficulties. That the colored man has a just and equal right, not only to life and liberty, but also to the means of grace and facilities for education, we not only admit, but most positively affirm.

"We are in duty bound to provide for and to secure to every class of our membership, so far as possible, a fair and equal opportunity in Church and school accommodations. And inso far as this is done our duty is performed, and the equal rights justly demanded of us thus fairly and fully conceded.

"Mixed congregations and mixed schools, may in some places, be most desirable, and best for all concerned. In other places, one class or the other, or both, may prefer separate congregations and separate schools.

"Equal rights to the best facilites for intellectual and spiritual culture, equal rights in the eligibility to every position of honor and trust, and equal rights in the exercise of a free and unconstrained choice in all social relations, is a principle at once American, Methodistic, and Scriptural. Therefore:

"*Resolved*, 1. That we most sincerely rejoice in the progress made in the work of education among our colored people in the South, and pledge ourselves to stand by and assist them in the further prosecution of this work, to the extent of our ability, and, so far as possible, to the extent of their need in this direction.

"2. That we heartily sympathize with our white membership in the South in their efforts to provide adequate educational facilities among themselves, and assure them of such co-operation and assistance as we may be able to render.

"3. That the question of separate or mixed schools we consider one of expediency, which is to be left to the choice and administration of those on the ground and more immediately concerned: *Provided*, there shall be no interference with the rights set forth in this preamble and these resolutions.

"4. That the entire educational work in the Southern States should be under the direction of one society.

"5. That in view of the great success of the Freedmen's Aid Society during the past four years in carrying forward the educational work in the South, this society ought to have the full charge of this work in that section.

"6. That the pastors, in presenting the claims of

this society in making appeals for funds, should state plainly that the work is among both races, and that all contributors should be allowed, whenever they may desire to do so, to designate where their gifts shall go."

REPORT NO. 2—ADOPTED MAY 23D.

" *Resolved*, That we fully appreciate the administration of the Freedmen's Aid Society during the past quadrennium."

REPORT NO. 4—ADOPTED MAY 23D.

" *Resolved*, That an appeal be made to the whole Church for half a million of dollars as a centennial offering to the great work of the Freedmen's Aid Society, and while through all other portions of the Church the usual agencies are employed in raising this amount, the Freedmen's Aid Society is hereby authorized and directed to organize and prosecute such financial effort among the conferences of the South."

REPORT NO. 5—ADOPTED MAY 23D.

" *Resolved*, That it would be unwise, by addition or otherwise, to change the name of the Freedmen's Aid Society."

REPORT NO. 6—ADOPTED MAY 23D.

" Your committee recommend the following changes in the Discipline, so that paragraph 1 shall read:

" ' For the mental and moral elevation of freedmen and others in the South, who have special claims upon the people of America for help in the work of Christian education.'

" Paragraph 310: 'It shall be the duty of each preacher in charge to present this subject to his congregation, or cause it to be presented, once each year in a

sermon or address; to aid in the diffusion of intelligence
in regard to the work of the society, and to use due diligence to collect the amount apportioned to his charge.
He shall report to the annual conference the sum collected, and the collections shall be published in a column
in the General Minutes, and in the Minutes of the annual conferences. In presenting the claims of this society, the preacher in charge shall state plainly that the
educational work of the society is among both white and
colored people."

FROM COMMITTEE ON STATE OF THE CHURCH, REPORT
No. 4—ADOPTED MAY 28TH.

" Your committee beg leave to submit the following
for your adoption, namely:

" *Resolved,* That this General Conference declares
the policy of the Methodist Episcopal Church to be, that
no member of any society within the Church shall be
excluded from public worship in any and every edifice
of the denomination, and no student shall be excluded
from instruction in any and every school under the supervision of the Church because of race, color or previous
condition of servitude."

FROM COMMITTEE ON FREEDMEN'S AID AND WORK IN THE
SOUTH, REPORT No. 7—ADOPTED MAY 28TH.

"The following statement of facts and conclusions respecting the work of our Church in the South is respectfully submitted by the Committee on Freedmen's Aid
and Work in the South:

" The growth of the Methodist Episcopal Church in
the Southern States since the close of the late war is
one of the marvels of modern Church history. Nine-

teen years ago—1864—the Church had within the border States of Maryland; West Virginia, Kentucky, and Missouri, 332 effective preachers, 71,037 white communicants, and 18,770 colored members. Now, in the sixteen former slave States and the District of Columbia, she has twelve conferences among the whites, with 693 effective preachers, and 170,710 communicants; thirteen conferences among the colored people, with 678 effective preachers, and 186,326 members. To these must be added three mixed conferences—two in Missouri and one in Florida—with 218 effective preachers, and 41,054 members, most of whom are white persons. These altogether make 28 annual conferences, with 1,589 effective preachers, and 398,090 communicants.

"This vast membership represents a following throughout the South of not less than 2,000,000 of people. Taking the South as a whole, this membership and following are divided about equally between the white and colored races—about 203,000 white members, and about 195,000 colored members. In the border States our strength is more largely among the white people; in our new Southern work, in the eleven States where the Church had nothing at the close of the war, our development has been larger among the colored people; but in these eleven States a white membership of 51,961 has been gathered. Over 3,500 new church-buildings have been erected on what was slave territory in 1860. The increase in Church parsonage property has been $6,282,723, and of membership 308,183. This is an average of over 20,000 member sand $350,000 annually.

"Nearly one-fourth of the entire membership of the Methodist Episcopal Church is now on what was slave territory, where, but a few years ago, the Church had no existence except in a few localities.

"Not less remarkable has been the educational development of our Church in the South. Since the late war, 48 colleges and seminaries have been established, and in these there are 194 instructors and over 6,000 young men and women. Of these schools 24 are among the colored people, and 24 among the white people. These latter have been established almost entirely by our white members themselves. These 48 institutions of learning are nearly one-third in number of all the institutions of learning of the Methodist Episcopal Church, and have in them 25 per cent of all persons being taught by our Church.

"The day of prosperity for the South is at hand, and the great questions affecting its civilization are being rapidly settled, and the spirit of fraternity and mutual helpfulness among all moral and educational forces at the South is rapidly prevailing. The presence and success of the Methodist Episcopal Church in the South have tended largely to these beneficent results; therefore,

" *Resolved*, 1. That as a General Conference we render thanks to God for the success that has attended the work of our Church in the Southern States, by which it has come to be permanently planted in every State in that section, so that we are now, in the matter of occupation as well as administration, a national Church.

" *Resolved*, 2. That we extend cordial greetings and benedictions to all our people, our teachers and pastors in the Southern States, and rejoice with them in their success, and sympathize with them in their labors; and we pledge to them, in behalf of the whole Church, the largest possible co-operation and help in every good word and work."

It can be seen at a glance that there was much conflict over the questions growing out of the relations of the two races within the Church in the South in that General Conference. Notwithstanding, it elected a representative colored man—W. H. Crogman, Professor of Ancient Languages in our Clark University, at Atlanta, Ga.—one of its secretaries; elected another—Rev. A. E. P. Albert, D. D., of Louisiana Conference—secretary of Committee on State of the Church; elected Rev. Marshall W. Taylor, D. D., editor-in-chief of one of the Church papers; yet it is difficult for some persons to understand clearly what *was meant* by the action taken touching the color question.

CHAPTER XII.

THE PROBLEM.

JUST what was intended by that General Conference touching this vexed question may be easily found out, if allowed to take as a basis the trite saying, "We have no way of judging the future but by the past." The declarations of the several General Conferences of our Church warrant us in declaring the following as her principles: "(1) God made of one blood all men for to dwell on the face of the earth; (2) God is no respecter of persons; but in every nation he that feareth him, and worketh righteousness, is accepted with him." The Methodist Episcopal Church is either founded upon and guided by the Word of God, or is nothing. The Church further declared: "(1) There is no word 'white' to discriminate against race or color known in our legislation; (2) Being of African descent does not prevent membership *with white men* in annual conferences; (3) Nor ordination at the same altars; (4) Nor appointment to presiding eldership; (5) Nor election to the General Conference; (6) Nor eligibility to the highest offices in the Church." (Journal, 1872, p. 373.) That the actions of that General Conference on the color question were enigmatical, the following will declare. The declaration of the General Conference of 1880 naturally led to, if it did not bring about, the entire discussion. The declaration was as follows:

"2. That under the phrase 'and others' of Article II, in the Constitution of the Freedmen's Aid Society, we see the way clear to aid the schools which have been established by our Church in the Southern States among the white people, and hereby ask the General Conference to recommend to the board of managers of this society to give such aid to these schools during the next quadrennium as can be done without embarrassment to the schools among the Freedmen."

If the words "to aid the schools which have been established by our Church in the Southern States among the white people," had been "the schools established in the Southern States among our white members, to be held sacredly for them to the exclusion of colored pupils," *it would have died on the spot, and been buried uncoffined, unknelled, and unknown.* It may be that a wrong construction is put on the former by the insertion of the latter words. If so, the sequel will so declare it. If not, then the phraseology was, and is, misleading. But it was adopted. What does it say? That the already existing exclusive schools for the whites, established within the Church in the Southern States, are to be fostered by the Freedmen's Aid Society, with the provision that, as a result, no embarrassment come to the schools for the freedmen.

Does not that provision imply *separate schools?*
We are trying simply to state facts as they exist,
without committal on the subject at this time.

In the last General Conference the second report
on Freedmen's Aid and Work in the South, offered
by Rev. J. C. Hartzell, D. D., indorsed the administration of the society during the quadrennium. If the discussion that preceded that General
Conference meant anything, it meant that it did not
indorse the Little Rock and Chattanooga enterprises *as projected.* The resolution offered by Rev.
C. O. Fisher, D. D., of Savannah Conference, and
adopted by that General Conference, without reference to any committee, declared it the sense of the
General Conference that color is no bar to any
right or privilege of office or membership in the
Church; that the propriety is recognized of so administering its affairs as "hereafter, as heretofore,
to secure the largest concession to individual preferences involving merely the social relations of
its members." No valid objection can be offered to
the last proposition. If it simply means that any
and every member of the Church has the right to
attend Church or schools wherever he pleases, without let or molestation *so far as law goes,* it is
simply another way of declaring the equality of
each and every member of the Church *so far as
privileges are concerned.* If the above supposition
is true, any objection on account of race, color, or
previous condition, raised by any one in authority

over Churches or schools under the auspices of the Church, is a flagrant violation of her law. We can conceive of but three valid reasons for any man offering such a resolution in a General Conference of a Church that has always conceded such, viz.: (1) To-show liberal-mindedness. (2) That there is no caste or race prejudice concealed among the colored members within the Methodist Episcopal Church that would cramp another member, or desires to insinuate itself upon the rights and prerogatives of others. (3) To prevent any unnecessary bickerings between the two races within the Church in the South. On top of the above came the report of the Committee on Freedmen's Aid and Work in the South. It declared the Church a friend to the colored man, and cited as evidence the work done by the society—twenty-four institutions of learning, connecting with it the expenditure of $1,250,000. That this management was (*a*) wise, (*b*) efficient, and (*c*) successful. Then came the other side of the question; the establishment of schools for the benefit of "the whites" within the Church in the South was (1) wise, (2) necessary, (3) gratifyingly successful, and had had a liberalizing effect upon public sentiment there that redounds to the advantage of the colored man; that it was a pity no more had been done, and it should be put upon a strong, permanent basis. Then came the *mixed school question.* As to the colored man, he was justly entitled to equal rights of not only "*life* and liberty," but to the means of grace and proper facilities for education; that the Church is bound to provide and secure to every class of its members, as far as possible, a fair and equal opportunity in Church and school accommodations. *As to mixed congregations and schools*, they "were in some places most desirable and best for all" (North, we presume), "in other places [South, we guess], one or the other, or both, may prefer separate congregations and schools." The question of equal rights is declared: (1) "To be the best facilities for intellectual and spiritual culture; (2) in the eligibility to every position of honor and trust; and (3) in the exercise of a free and unconstrained choice in all social relations." This was declared "a principle at once American, Methodistic, and Scriptural." Then come the resolutions. The first rejoices in the work done among and for the colored people, supports a pledge to stand by and support it to the extent of its needs, measured by the ability of the Church. The next two resolutions are the most objectionable offered, viz.:

"2. That we heartily sympathize with our white membership in the South in their efforts to provide adequate educational facilities *among themselves*, and assure them of such co-operation and assistance as we may be able to render.

"3. That the question of separate or mixed schools we consider one of expediency, which is to be left to the choice and administration of those on the ground and more immediately concerned: *Provided*, there shall be no interference with the rights set forth in this preamble and these resolutions."

Let us scrutinize these a moment. The General Conference, by the adoption of these two resolutions, sympathized with an effort "to provide adequate educational facilities *among themselves*"—the white members of our Church in the South. If disposed to hunt objections, we would say they had already 'adequate educational facilities," as a result of the educational work done by the Freedmen's Aid Society, if they would have accepted them, and without additional efforts on their part. Again, the General Conference, by its action, desired to "assure them of such co-operation and assistance as we may be able to render." It may be short-sightedness or ignorance to say so, but the way these resolutions read they certainly seem not only not to object to discrimination, but to *encourage it.*

By the second resolution the question of mixed or separate schools was declared: (1) "One of expediency, to be left to the choice and administration of those on the ground, and more immediately concerned." That which is expedient, Webster declares "a means to an end." Was it so intended in that resolution? "Those on the ground and more immediately concerned" were undoubtedly the trustees, teachers, and patrons of the schools among the whites in our Church. (2) "*Provided*, there shall be no interference with the rights set forth in this—

the foregoing—preamble and these resolutions." The preamble declared: "(1) Equal rights to the best facilities for intellectual and spiritual culture, equal rights in the eligibility to every position of honor and trust, and equal rights in the exercise of a free and unconstrained choice in all social relations as a principle at once American, Methodistic, and Scriptural." Now let us put *this* and *that* together; who is to decide what are "the best facilities for intellectual and spiritual culture?" According to the principle of expediency—"the means to an end"—undoubtedly it must be decided by "those on the ground and more immediately concerned." Now, the question as to whether the contributors—the majority of the most liberal contributors—are "more immediately concerned," we do not stop to say. Having completed the addition, what do we find as a rational conclusion? What are we to understand by "the exercise of a free and *unconstrained* choice in all social relations?" Webster says: "The word constrain comes from the Latin *constringere*. This is composed of *con* and *stringere*, to draw tight, to strain; a strong, binding force; to hold back by force." The word used is *unconstrained*. I suppose we can conclude it means without constraint. The question naturally arises, Had there been any *constraint* in our work in the South? If so, at what point? Touching what phase of the work? Whatever constraint the work in the South has been laboring under, the Church was responsible for it.   Was it that "race, color, nor previous condition" should be a bar to the full and equal rights of its members in Church, school, or office?   There must have been some *constraint*, or the word "unconstrained" is meaningless, as used. But whatever constrained choice existed previously, it was so intended, and that resolution did abrogate, if it has any force at all.   What did "those on the ground and more immediately concerned" understand it to mean?   Rather, what naturally grew out of it?

THE CHATTANOOGA EPISODE.

An educational convention was held in Athens, Tennessee, in 1882, composed of delegates from nearly all our conferences, composed exclusively of white-people, for the purpose of "looking after the educational interests of the work among the whites." The question of the establishment of a university for the benefit of the white members and patrons of our Church in the central South was decided upon, and a plan was adopted for the co-operation of the conferences and Freedmen's Aid Society in founding and locating the same, subject to the approval of the conferences.   "This action was heartily and unanimously concurred in by the pastors and educators among the whites."   Considering their *modus operandi* "the best for intellectual and spiritual culture," as well as the most direct and practical "exercise of a free and unconstrained choice

in all social relations, as a principle at once American, Methodistic, and Scriptural," it was accepted by
"those on the ground and more immediately concerned," and "left to their choice and administration." Chattanooga was chosen as the seat of the
great university in the central South for whites.
Now, if no other reason could have been given for
that choice, the fact that from Lookout Mountain
the rebel soldiers were driven by General Grant
during the late civil war was sufficient for historical
prestige. The relevancy of the following quota-
tion from Ridpath's History, giving an account of
the movements of General Grant around that city
during the civil war, may not at once appear to
all. He says: "General Grant, being promoted to
the chief command, assumed the direction of affairs
at Chattanooga. General Sherman also arrived with
his divisions, and offensive operations were at once
renewed. A position seemingly more impregnable
could hardly be conceived of." Chattanooga having
been selected as the place for "a central university
for the South," fourteen acres of ground, costing
thirty-one thousand dollars, were purchased, and a
magnificent structure, costing forty thousand dollars, was erected thereon. Of this amount the citizens of the city contributed fifteen thousand dollars.
It has been suggested that some of the contributors
of that sum, at least, gave their money with the
distinct understanding that the university was to
be for the benefit of *white pupils exclusively.* This

intelligence was not received from the managers of the Freedmen's Aid Society, as such; so that, if at all, it may have been received from some of "those on the ground and more immediately concerned." When the university opened, September 15, 1886, everything looked hopeful, indeed, to "those on the ground and more immediately concerned." But soon it was found that the brightness of those prospects was but the silver lining of an approaching cloud. Two incidents happened shortly afterward that gave that institution more prominence than any other two incidents in its history can possibly ever do. Among the students who applied for admittance into the institution were four colored youths of that city or vicinity. The trustees of the institution refused to admit them. The board of trustees, by contract with the Freedmen's Aid Society, reserved the right, not only to appoint the teachers, but to purchase the property whenever they became able to pay back seventy-five thousand dollars to the society, and give the university an endowment of two hundred thousand dollars. But one of the incidents happened before anything was said about the rejection of colored students. One of the professors in the university—Professor Caulkins—met and was introduced to the pastor of our colored Church in Chattanooga, Rev. B. H. Johnson, by Rev. Dr. T. C. Carter, and he refused to shake hands with or recognize him "on general principles," as he declared. The following, which appeared in the *Western Christian Advocate,* is explicit and to the point:

PROFESSOR CAULKINS.

"In another column will be found a statement from the executive committee of the Freedmen's Aid Society, concerning the episode in which Professor Caulkins and the Rev. B. H. Johnson were the principal participants. It will be seen that the executive committee acted in the case with great promptness and decision, the committee's first action having been taken within four days after the first rumor of the case reached any member of the committee.

"The following extract from the minutes of the meeting of October 26th will show the precise action which was taken at that early day:

"'Dr. Bayliss moved that the corresponding secretary be instructed to ascertain whether it be true that Professor Caulkins, of Chattanooga University, refused to shake hands with one of our pastors in Chattanooga because he was a Negro; and also in a series of articles made disparaging remarks, and used insulting language in reference to the colored people, and that if these rumors should prove true, the president shall lay the matter before the local board, and ask for his resignation. Carried.'

"If any one should be inclined to the opinion that the inquiry was not prosecuted as rapidly as it should have been, it must be considered that immediately after the sub-committee was appointed, Bishop Walden was necessarily in attendance at the meeting of the bishops; that Bishop Walden, Dr. Cranston, and the editor of this paper, all of whom are members of the executive

MEHARRY MEDICAL COLLEGE, NASHVILLE, TENN.

committee, were necessarily at the meeting of the General Missionary Committee in New York, which was held just after the bishops' meeting; that the president of the society was immediately afterward called to Philadelphia to the annual meeting of the Church Extension Committee, and that the annual meeting of the Freedmen's Aid Society was held in Boston on the 23d of November, at which it was necessary for both the president and secretary of the society to be present. Thus the month of November was crowded full of travel and work, and it was next to impossible to have a meeting of the executive committee until December 1st, when a meeting was held. The general history of the inquiry is given in the 'Statement,' and need not be repeated here.

"We have reason to believe that the board of trustees of the university will act in the case without delay, and we are therefore not disposed at this time to enter upon any discussion of it. Our views are clear, and if it shall become necessary we shall have no hesitation in justifying them. Professor Caulkins's moral character is not involved in the case. That he is a fine scholar and teacher, and that he means to be a gentleman, we fully believe. At the same time we also believe that his views and feelings upon what is known as the 'color question,' or the 'Negro question,' are such as to make him an improper person to hold a position as teacher in a school officially connected with the Freedmen's Aid Society. We say this after having heard the case freely stated by Mr. Johnson, Professor Caulkins, and Dr. Carter, and after hearing the declarations of others who have knowledge of Professor Caulkins's views. At this time, however, we do not think it necessary to discuss the statements which we have heard, and thus prove the justness of our conclusions. The trustees of the university have access to all the parties interested, and we prefer to leave the case in their hands for final adjudication, as they constitute the body which has the power to dismiss teachers. We only add that the Freedmen's Aid Society of the Methodist Episcopal Church can not, and in our judgment will not, continue in its employ any person who is capable of showing disrespect, under any circumstances, to a colored person because he is colored. The Methodist Episcopal Church is the exponent of a nobler sentiment, and will not stultify herself by allowing one of her great benevolent societies to employ as a teacher in one of our schools, any man who stands for the views which the country has inherited from the institution of slavery; and in this the Freedmen's Aid Society is in exact harmony with the views of the Church. The black man is a man, and the fact must be recognized."

STATEMENT

FROM THE EXECUTIVE COMMITTEE OF THE FREEDMEN'S AID SOCIETY IN THE CASE OF PROFESSOR CAULKINS.

"It has been widely published that Professor Caulkins, of Chattanooga University, Tennessee, a school officially connected with the Freedmen's Aid Society of the Methodist Episcopal Church, and built and supported for the most part by funds from its treasury, refused to shake hands with the Rev. B. H. Johnson, pastor of one of the Methodist Episcopal Churches of Chattanooga, and that he refused the proffered hand of Mr. Johnson because Mr. Johnson is a colored man. It has also been reported that Professor Caulkins, in conversation with the Rev. Dr. Carter, immediately after the alleged insult to Mr. Johnson, used words which indicated his personal prejudice against the Negro race.

"In view of the wide circulation of these accusations, the executive committee of the Freedmen's Aid Society makes the following statement of facts:

"The first report of the case was made to some members of the executive committee about the 22d of October, and the president of the society, Bishop Walden, did not hear of it until the 25th. On the 26th a meeting of the executive committee was held, the president of the society being in the chair, and at this meeting Dr. Rust, the corresponding secretary, was directed to ascertain the facts in the case, and, if the disparaging rumors concerning Professor Caulkins should prove to be true, Bishop Walden was directed to lay the matter before the board of trustees of the university, and ask for Professor Caulkins's resignation. The vote of the committee upon this resolution was unanimous. Bishop Walden went immediately to New York to attend the bishops' meeting and other annual meetings.

"Dr. Rust secured written statements from Dr. Carter, Mr. Johnson, and Professor Caulkins. At a meeting of the executive committee, December 1st, held on the bishop's return from the East, the matter was called up, but no formal report was made, it being the wish of the committee that Bishop Walden should see the parties on the ground, and ascertain, so far as possible, all the facts bearing upon the case. He presented his report to the executive committee, Monday, December 20th, the earliest date practicable after he had secured a meeting of the parties in Chattanooga. Pending the consideration of the report, the committee adjourned to Thursday, December 23d.

"The annual meeting of the board of managers of the Freedmen's Aid Society was held on the 21st of December, and this case was called up, and by resolution was left to the executive committee to take such action as the facts might require.

" Dr. Carter and Professor Caulkins being present on the 23d, each, by request of the committee, made a full statement. In view of these statements it was deemed best to have personal statements from other parties, and the committee requested the presence of Mr. Johnson, President Lewis, Dr. Manker, and Mr. J. H. Bowman at an adjourned meeting held Tuesday, December 28th. These were all present at this meeting except Mr. Bowman, and each made a statement before the committee.

"The committee spared neither time nor patient labor in investigating the case, and after mature deliberation, the entire committee being present, adopted the following:

" '1. That we, the executive committee of the Freedmen's Aid Society, strongly condemn an insult or discourtesy to a colored person on account of color or previous condition; that we hold that no person who entertains sentiments either inimical or prejudicial to the colored people, as such, should have a position of trust in any institution of our Church; that we do unqualifiedly condemn the refusal or failure of Professor Caulkins to shake hands with Rev. B. H. Johnson, and deplore the results of what Professor Caulkins claims to have been carelessness on his part.

"'2. That a majority of this executive committee is convinced that Professor Caulkins did intentionally refuse to shake hands with Rev. B. H. Johnson; that he does entertain sentiments that unfit him for a position in a school with which our Freedmen's Aid Society is officially connected, and that he should be asked to resign at once.

"'3. That inasmuch as the power to dismiss teachers from the Chattanooga University is vested by the charter in its board of trustees, we, the executive committee of the Freedmen's Aid Society, refer the foregoing statements and conclusions to said board of trustees, and respectfully request a speedy decision in the matter, and that the decision be placed before the Church at the earliest day practicable.

"'Attest: J. M. WALDEN, President.

"'T. H. PEARNE, Secretary.'"

When the foregoing action of the board of managers was communicated to the trustees, they refused to comply.

The following from the *Western Christian Advocate* has the right ring:

PROFESSOR CAULKINS'S CASE.

"We learn that the trustees of the Chattanooga University decline to comply with the request of the executive committee of the Freedmen's Aid Society as to the removal of Professor Caulkins. We learn this with much regret, because one result will be a disturbance of the harmonious relations which should exist between the trustees and the executive committee. We do not see how the committee can possibly recede from its position. When the matter was sent back by the trustees for further consideration, and some new facts were submitted, it was the conviction of the committee that the new facts made the case against the professor stronger than before, and the request for his removal was more prompt and emphatic in the second instance than in the first. As we have already said, we are fully satisfied that Professor Caulkins means to be a gentleman; but a man who could, under any possible circumstances, say such things about the Negro as Professor Caulkins certainly has said, and act toward a colored minister as he did act toward Mr. Johnson, is not a proper person to occupy the position of teacher in a Freedmen's Aid Society school, and the effort of the trustees to retain him can accomplish no desirable results. The professor ought to resign, and thus end the controversy over his case. That the five trustees who voted to retain him in the university are sincere in their motives we do not for one moment doubt, but they certainly do not see the case as the great mass of the members of the Methodist Episcopal Church see it, and their position is clearly untenable. Professor Caulkins should not be permitted to remain in that institution. If nothing else can be done, notice should at once be given to terminate the contract between the Freedmen's Aid Society and the trustees, and at the earliest practicable moment a new administration should be inaugurated. One mission of the Methodist Episcopal Church in the South is to teach a better theory concerning the Negro than the South has heretofore held, and it is wholly incongruous for us to employ as teachers in the South men who hold upon this particular subject opinions which we are there to destroy. However pure the motives of the trustees may be, and we have no suspicion of them, their course is not wise, and if persisted in will lead to serious consequences. We hope they will reconsider their action before the evils are precipitated upon us which must otherwise inevitably result.

MIXED SCHOOLS—LET US BE WISE.

"It will be a very disastrous state of things if, while the Chattanooga University is under discussion, the collections for the Freedmen's Aid Society shall be postponed. The society is in debt now, and funds must be supplied or its work will be crippled, and in the not distant future will have to be suspended. More money should be given this year than in any previous year.

"No change in the administration of the society has been inaugurated. The colored work and the white work are going on now just as they have done for years, only more successfully than ever before. There have never been any colored students in our white schools in the South, and the last General Conference knew this fact, and approved the administration of the Freedmen's Aid Society. One of our contemporaries says that colored students can find a way into Grant Memorial University, at Athens, Tennessee; but that is certainly a mistake. We can not learn that one colored student has ever been in that school, nor do we believe that one would be admitted there. Our white schools in the South are for whites exclusively, and have been so from the beginning.

"We do not now discuss the main question at issue, but we do say that, in our judgment, those in charge of the Freedmen's Aid Society have been administering the trust committed to them just as they administered it before the last General Conference, and as they understood the instructions given them by that General Conference. The *Freedmen's Aid Society* has never excluded colored students from white schools. Certain colored persons who applied for admittance to Chattanooga University were refused by the local authorities, and only a few days ago the matter was referred to the officers of the Freedmen's Aid Society, when a meeting of the board of managers was at at once called to consider the question. So far as we know, this is the first action of the kind in the history of the society. What conclusion the board will reach we do not know, and do not now care to conjecture, although our own views upon the whole subject are entirely clear. We do not believe that under the action of the General Conference of 1884 those students can be rightfully refused admittance to the university, and whatever the results may be, the General Conference itself must bear the responsibility for them. We confess our profound conviction, and our painful fear, that if this view shall be adopted and acted upon, our entire educational work among the whites of the South will be imperiled. The prejudice against the introduction of colored students to our white schools in the South is more violent than it would be against the appointment of a colored man as pastor of Trinity Church, Chicago; or, if such a thing were possible, of Plymouth Church, Brooklyn. We do not believe that mixed schools in the South, generally, are yet possible, and this fact has influenced the action of the General Conference upon this whole subject. It is barely possible that if that body had fully appreciated the gravity of the situation, the resolution of May 28, 1884, setting forth the policy of the Church, would not have been adopted. However this may be, to us the action of the Conference admits of but one interpretation, and when a student knocks at the door of any one of our schools, the opening of the door must not depend upon the color of the applicant. Whether the action of the conference be wise or unwise is a very different question; but this is our interpretation of what it did.

"For the present, however, we are anxious that the regular collections for the society shall be taken, so that its growing and glorious work may not be crippled. If the collections cease, the colored work will be destroyed. Our white people in the South can do something on educational lines for themselves, but our colored people can do little, if anything; and when the people of the North fail to send in the money, the schools for the colored people must inevitably close. Let no angry criticism of the society result in robbery of Christ's poor.

"We trust the Church will see the case just as it is, and not rush to a conclusion which will endanger our hitherto prosperous work in the South. The board of managers of the society can be trusted to do what is right and wise. Let the collections be taken as usual, and send the money in promptly, and wait in patience for a deliverance from the board of managers. We do not need angry passion just now, but coolness, deliberation, wisdom, and the fear and love of God. Let these virtues prevail, and no disaster will befall us."

The trustees of Chattanooga University having refused to ask Professor Caulkins to resign his position in the institution, the *Western Christian Advocate* reported, editorially and otherwise, the following, which we insert in full, because the editor was present during all the deliberations of the body, and was chairman of the sub-committee which prepared the statements and resolutions which were considered, amended, and adopted:

"The action of the board of managers of the Freedmen's Aid Society will be found in another column, and will be read very widely and with much care. The editor of the *Western* was present during all the deliberations of the body, and was chairman of the sub-committee which prepared the statements and resolutions which were considered, amended, and adopted. He is, therefore, in a position to know how the board reached its conclusions, and the spirit of all the discussions. The work was done prayerfully and carefully, and with profound appreciation of the principles involved and of the possible results of the action taken. The board understood that it was dealing, directly or indirectly, with the entire work of our Church in the South; for, as matter of fact, the fate of our Churches in that part of the country is more closely related to the fate of our schools than most persons think. It took a broad view of the whole subject, and after many hours of deliberation on three successive days, adopted the deliverance which is now laid before the Church. What its statements and resolutions are, the reader will learn by personal examination of them. They are easily understood. No adroit play is attempted upon the word 'policy,' nor is the resolution of May 28, 1884, treated as a 'barren ideality,' The board adopted the view of the whole question which was set forth editorially in these columns some weeks ago. That the General Conference intended to continue separate schools for the two races is entirely clear to us, and that it also intended that those schools should not be absolutely exclusive as to either race, is equally clear. This is the view taken by the board of managers, and seems to us wholly correct.

"We believe it will harmonize with the thought of the Church. We do not believe there is a general disposition to destroy, or even to cripple, our work among the whites of the South; on the contrary, the remarkable success of that work is a cause of joy to the great majority of our people, and they are ready to aid and extend it. But there is a conviction that the last General Conference intended to utter a practical protest against that caste spirit which has so long trampled upon the Negro race; and there is also a conviction that the age is outgrowing that prejudice, and that in this advance toward ideal gospel fraternity the Church should lead the age. The board shared this conviction, and voiced its opinion in an interpretation of the action of the General Conference which none can misunderstand. What the effect will be upon our work in the South no one can foretell. It is possible that our schools in that section may all become schools of colored people; for it is just possible that if colored students shall be admitted to what are now called white schools, all the white students will be foolish enough to leave them. This is prophesied and desired by some who wish us evil, and is feared by some who wish us well, and some of our enemies are already standing ready to laugh at our confusion.

"We hope for better things. We have no idea that large numbers of colored students will apply for admittance to these schools; for while they do not enjoy being excluded from them by law, they prefer the schools which are attended mostly by their own people, and which, as matter of fact, are among the best in the South. We do not believe that they will purposely embarrass the work among the whites by insisting upon their rights under the action of the General Conference as interpreted by the board of managers. We are free to say that we hope they will not do it. Whatever the result is to be, however, the General Conference took the action which the board has now interpreted, and which, in our judgment, it could not consistently interpret in any other way.

"We believe the Church will approve what the board has done, not only by words but by increased contributions to the cause. The society is heavily in debt, and while it has a very large amount of property, and is in no sense bankrupt, it ought to have an annual income of two hundred and fifty thousand dollars.

"The action of the board shows how unjust much of the criticism of the society has been. This is the first and only time in its history when it has been called upon to interpret General Conference action upon this subject, and it speaks promptly and clearly. We never had any doubt as to what it would say when an opportunity for utterance should be given, and we prophesied editorially what the result would be. That time has come; the voice of the society has been heard; and it is now in order for hostile critics to confess how they have wronged a society which ran to the help of the freedman before the roar of the battle which made him free had died away, and has done more since, with the amount of money at its command, than any other benevolent society in the world.

"We trust that those who are particularly interested in our work among the whites of the South will not lose heart. A better day is dawning. It would be a poor tribute to our work during the last quarter of a century if the introduction of a few colored students into our schools for whites should break the institutions down. Have we really made so little progress that six colored students at Chattanooga would drive out two hundred white students? We can hardly believe it. When three chase a hundred, the three must be very strong or the hundred very weak. We believe our white work will go on, and that this action of the board will strengthen the society and increase its success."

ACTION OF THE BOARD OF MANAGERS
OF THE FREEDMEN'S AID SOCIETY OF THE METHODIST EPISCOPAL CHURCH.

"The board of managers of the Freedmen's Aid Society of the Methodist Episcopal Church, at the call of its executive committee, convened at its office in Cincinnati, Ohio, February 22, 1887, the following members being present: J. M. Walden, Amos Shinkle, M. B. Hagans, R. S. Rust, J. C. Hartzell, T. H. Pearne, Earl Cranston, W. L. Hypes, D. J. Starr, H. Liebhart, W. F. Boyd, J. H. Bayliss, W. P. Stowe, Joseph Courtney, Isaac W. Joyce, Bidwell Lane, J. M. Shumpert, E. W. S. Hammond, J. W. Dale, J. D. Shutt, F. S. Hoyt, J. Krehbiel—two members being absent, namely: F. C.

Holliday, through personal illness, and Edward Sargent, on account of affliction in his family.

"The following was submitted for consideration:

EXTRACT FROM MINUTES OF EXECUTIVE COMMITTEE OF CHATTANOOGA UNIVERSITY.

"'WHEREAS, At the opening of the Chattanooga University, September 15, 1886, certain colored persons applied to the faculty for admission as students in the institution; and

"'WHEREAS, Certain other colored persons residing in Athens, Tennessee, have applied for admission at the opening of the second term, now about to commence; and

"'WHEREAS, It has been again and again definitely and clearly stated by the proper authorities of the Church, and from the beginning has been well understood by all concerned, that the Chattanooga University was designed for the education of white pupils, and was not intended to be a mixed school; and

"'WHEREAS, It is well known that first-class institutions, well equipped and provided by the Church especially for the education of people of color, are within easy reach of all such persons who really desire to avail themselves of their benefits, so that they are in no proper sense dependent on this institution for education; and

"'WHEREAS, We are confident that, in the present state of society in the South, the admission of colored students to the Chattanooga University would, on the one hand, be fatal to the prosperity of the institution, and defeat the very object proposed by the Church in the establishment of the school; and, on the other hand, would not only be unproductive of good results to the

colored students so admitted, but would excite prejudice
and passion, alienate the races, and prove especially det-
rimental to the interests of the colored people; and

"'Whereas, This very question of mixed schools
has, by the General Conference itself, been declared to
be "one of expediency, which is to be left to the choice
and administration of those on the ground and more
immediately concerned;" therefore, be it

"' *Resolved*, That we deem it inexpedient to admit
colored students to the university, and that the faculty
be instructed to administer accordingly.

"'Adopted January 4, 1887.'

"In view of this action, and after full consideration
of the whole subject, the board of managers adopts the
following statements and resolutions:

"1. The last General Conference authorized the
Freedmen's Aid Society to aid in the maintenance and
establishment of separate schools among the white members of our Church in the South. It did this by recognizing the separate white schools then existing in the
South as entitled to aid; by directing the Freedmen's Aid
Society to co-operate in maintaining and establishing such
schools; by approving the aid this society had already
extended to these schools; and by directing the pastors
when taking collections for the Freedmen's Aid Society
to 'state plainly that the educational work of the
society is among both white and colored people.' There
can, therefore, be no doubt that it was the intention to
continue separate schools in connection with the Freedmen's Aid Society; yet, in the judgment of this board
of managers, it is in harmony with the prevailing sentiment of the last General Conference to interpret its

action as being designed to forbid the exclusion of any student 'from instruction in any and every school under the supervision of the Church because of race, color, or previous condition of servitude;' and we hereby declare that no pupil should be excluded on account of race, color, or previous condition of servitude, from instruction in the schools under the control of this Freedmen's Aid Society or aided by its funds, under the authority of the last General Conference.

"In the above interpretation of the action of the last General Conference touching this general principle of equality, it is the judgment of this board that it was not the expectation of the General Conference that any advantage would be taken of its deliverance on this subject by persons or parties interested in embarrassing the work of our Church, or of this society; and, therefore, we trust that the parties directly interested in its practical application will so act as to promote good-will and insure the usefulness of all the schools under the care of this society. We also call attention to, and emphasize, the following action of the last General Conference, viz:

" 'The establishment of schools for the benefit of our white membership in the South we believe to have been a wise and necessary measure. Their success has been gratifying. The beneficial results have not been confined to those immediately interested, but their liberalizing effects upon public sentiment have greatly redounded to the advantage of our colored people. We regret that for so great and important a work so little has been done by the Church, and we desire most emphatically to give expression to our conviction that the time has come when this portion of our educational work should be strengthened and placed upon a strong and permanent basis, as its importance certainly demands.'

"2. WHEREAS, It appears from the above action of the Chattanooga University that certain students were denied admission to that institution for the sole reason that they were persons of African descent; and

"WHEREAS, In the judgment of this board there is neither in the charter of the Chattanooga University, nor in the contract between said university and the Freedmen's Aid Society, anything authorizing the exclusion of students from instruction in said institution on account of color or race; and as the General Conference, on May 28, 1884, did, as its last utterance on this question, declare ' the policy of the Methodist Episcopal Church to be, that . . . no student shall be excluded from instruction in any and every school under the supervision of the Church because of race, color, or previous condition of servitude ;' therefore,

"*Resolved*, That we disapprove the exclusion of those students for the reason assigned; and hereby instruct our executive committee to use all proper means at its command to induce the trustees of the Chattanooga University to rescind the order by which those students were refused instruction in that institution.

"3. WHEREAS, The executive committee of the Chattanooga University has declined to ask for the resignation of Professor Wilford Caulkins as a member of the faculty of that institution, although such action has been twice requested by the executive committee of this board; therefore,

"*Resolved*, By the board of managers of the Freedmen's Aid Society, that we approve the course of our executive committee in seeking to secure the resignation of Professor Caulkins; and, while carefully and respectfully considering the reasons urged by the executive committee of the Chattanooga University for his retention, it is our conviction that the best interests of the society and the Church demand his removal.

"4. WHEREAS, Harmony between this board and the Chattanooga University is essential to the effective working of the said university; therefore,

"*Resolved*, That if the Chattanooga University fail to secure the resignation of Professor Wilford Caulkins, to take effect at a date not later than the close of the present school term, and so to modify its action as not to exclude from instruction in that institution students on account race or color; *i. e.*, if the said university fail in either of these particulars, we hereby instruct our executive committee to secure by agreement, if possible, with the trustees of said university, the immediate termination of the contract between the Chattanooga University and the Freedmen's Aid Society; and, in case a termination of said contract be not secured by mutual agreement, in either of the contingencies named above, to notify the trustees of the Chattanooga University, within sixty days from this 24th day of February, 1887, of the termination of the contract as provided in the same.

"Done by the Board of Managers of the Freedmen's Aid Society of the Methodist Episcopal Church, at its office in Cincinnati, Ohio, this 24th day of February, A. D. 1887.

"J. M. WALDEN, President.

"Attest: T. H. PEARNE, Secretary."

CHAPTER XIII.

THEORY AND PRACTICE—A GENERAL DISCUSSION.

WHILE the board of managers was in session, as well as before and afterward, a general discussion, pro and con, was going on. We give but a few of the many expressions of opinion on the subject; enough, however, for one to form an intelligent opinion touching the real intention of the Church. If it should appear to any one that the actions taken by the last General Conference were ambiguous, not to say plainly contradictory, not only with themselves but the past record of the Church, it will occasion no surprise. The *Central Christian Advocate*, at St. Louis, spoke editorially, March 2d, as follows:

THEORY AND PRACTICE.

"The decision of those who are in charge of the new university at Chattanooga, erected under the direction of, and out of the funds collected for, the Freedmen's Aid Society, that colored students shall not be admitted to its benefits, has brought the Methodist Episcopal Church face to face with certain questions which only the next General Conference can settle. But in the meantime it is wise to examine the questions involved from every point of view, and, if possible, thoroughly comprehend the situation; for, in matters of this kind, we are apt to form opinions before we have canvassed the whole field, and to make accusations that will not stand investigation. That there are differences of opinion in regard to the intention of the last General Conference in its legislation on the subject under discussion, no one can doubt. There were those in that body who understood that certain action in which they had a part established the rule that no distinctions founded on race or color should be made under any circumstances in any of our schools. But there are others who as certainly understood that there would probably be circumstances where the success of our educational work in the South would depend upon setting apart some of the schools there exclusively for the whites. It is not a difference of opinion that admits any suspicion of a lack of honesty or piety in either party, much less the accusation of trickery or intentional wrong-doing. And it will be found, we think, after proper consideration, that these differences may be easily explained; that they are simply the differences of opinion which always arise in the transformation and development of society between the party of theory and that of experience and practice.

"The Methodist Episcopal Church holds to the theory that God 'hath made of one blood all nations of men;' that they were all involved in the fall, and all have been redeemed by Christ, and may become partakers of the same faith and eternal inheritance. We hold that the social and civil distinctions which prevail in society are of men, not of God. 'There is neither Jew nor Greek, there is neither bond nor free, there is neither male nor female, for ye are all one in Christ Jesus.' It is not possible—so at least it appears to us—

to conceive of Christ as recognizing these distinctions except to condemn them, and to show his sympathy for the oppressed or degraded party. The conviction and faith of the Methodist Episcopal Church is as strong, and her practice as nearly in accord with her faith, as that of any Protestant Church; but her faith and practice are not, and never have been, in harmony in regard to the colored people. The simple fact is, that wherever the colored people have become Methodists, and are found in any considerable number, they have been formed into separate societies; when a number of societies have been formed they have been organized into a separate district, and in the end into separate conferences. The line of procedure has been the same in the North, where slavery has not prevailed for generations, and the rights of the colored people are fully recognized, as in the South where the prejudice against them is the greatest. So that there is not to-day, so far as we know, a single colored Church, able to support a pastor, in charge of a white pastor. There is not a society of whites, in any condition of poverty or ignorance, served by a colored pastor. There are a few districts of colored societies served by white presiding elders, but not one white district by a colored presiding elder. And we do not believe there is a society of whites anywhere in the Church that have asked for or would receive a colored pastor, whatever might be his grade of talent. They would not object to hear one of this description preach, and they would treat him with consideration, but they would hardly ask him to become their pastor.

"We believe this to be a fair statement of the situation. It does not mean that we intend to be unjust or unchristian, nor that we harbor secret prejudice against our colored brethren, but simply that the condition of things about us makes it impossible, as we say, to put our theory in practice. We are not hypocrites, nor are we consciously faint at heart in contending for the equal rights of all men; but we have learned that the leaven of Christianity has not yet leavened society. We find our theory and the practical reason not in accord, and we follow reason. For we are not propagating a theory but engaged in obtaining actual benefits for men. The object we have in view is itself a step towards the overthrow of error and sin and prejudice. It is not a surrender, but accepting what we can not at once change that we may yet reach the object in view.

"Some one, however, may say, But what about the schools? The school is not a necessity in the same sense that the Church is; and if people prefer to remain ignorant rather than obtain education under certain circumstances, let them take the responsibility. This means, we take it, that we shall not undertake to do anything towards the education of the whites in the South. And yet it is by education alone that this prejudice which we are asked to combat is to be removed. Those in charge of the Chattanooga University have not, we think, taken counsel of their fears in this matter, but have an intelligent conviction of their duty under the circumstances. And yet it might have been worth the experiment to have made the test, and let the Church know exactly the difficulty which confronts a company of men who have at heart the welfare alike of white and colored. But right here is where the difference of opinion comes in—where theory and practice come in collision; the one party is no more willing to yield than the other. Whether we can maintain a condition in our Church schools which we have failed to maintain in the Church—where prejudice should have less influence than anywhere else—is, to say the least, problematical. And the question which will come before the next General Conference is: Shall we undertake to establish a condition of affairs in the South which we have utterly failed to establish in the North under more favorable circumstances."

March 2d the following appeared in the *Northwestern Christian Advocate*, from the pen of A. Wheeler, D. D.:

"The refusal of the Chattanooga University to admit the colored students who made application for reception into its halls has exposed them to severe criticism, not to say malediction. A reconstruction of its administration is loudly called for, more in harmony with the policy and principles of the Church. The suggestion that the great wrong done should at least be divided with another authority seems not to have occurred to any of the horrified accusers living a thousand miles away from the scene of trouble. Is this as it ought to be? Is it justice? Is it fair play?

"In this transaction two things claim attention,—the principle underlying it, and its application. As to the principle: The General Conference of 1876 indorsed the principle of separate conferences and societies. Is the principle of separation right in the house of God, and wrong in the house of learning? The General Conference of 1884 recognized the principle as appropriate also to our schools in the South. Was this done as an abstraction, with no expectation of a concrete application? If so, it ought to have been known. If the principle is wrong, it is but just that condemnation fall upon the General Conferences enacting it, and moral cowardice to visit such indignation on the Chattanooga agents of the Church carrying out a principle ordained by the highest authority of the Church—a principle to be carried into operation under certain contingencies.

"The application of the principle is the other matter to be considered. Who was to apply it? Somebody in Detroit or Boston, or the trustees and faculties intrusted with the care of the institutions? To ask the question is to answer it. A mistake in the application of the principle in a given case might be made, but are those making it to be adjudged worse sinners than those upon whom the tower of Siloam fell therefor? If those applying a principle mistakenly be worthy of death, of how much sorer punishment shall they be thought worthy who gave them the principle to apply? But the General Conference of 1884 declared the policy of the Methodist Episcopal Church to be . . . that 'no student shall be excluded from instruction in any and every school under the supervision of the Church because of race, color, or previous condition of servitude.' What of it? Had that deliverance the force of an enactment? Was it true to history? Will any claim it to be history? Who have declared it? When and where was the declaration made? Had such a policy been carried into execution? When? By whom? Had it been at Athens or Little Rock, the only other schools established for whites at the South?

"The statement never ought to have been made by the committee, nor indorsed by the General Conference. The policy of exclusion had never been adopted, it is true, but the trend of the legislation of the Church since 1876 had been in the direction of separation in worship and education, under certain conditions. To institute such legislation, and then visit unsparing indignation on those whose duty it is to apply it, is neither just nor manly, unless the application has been made in a way faithless to a committed trust. I am not defending the principle of separation in conferences or schools. It may be wrong. If it is, let us say so and abandon it; but till we do abandon it, let us not blame those for whose benefit it was adopted for using it when the conditions for its use are present. Nor let us conclude that one of the qualifications for judging conditions is distance from the scene of action, and that competency is in proportion to remoteness. Let those of us who voted the principle, if it be blameworthy, bear our part of the blame, and not saddle it all off upon the Chattanooga authorities. Let us hold them responsible for a misuse of it only. To legislate a principle that was never to be used would be simply a mockery."

March 9th the following contribution, which appeared in the columns of the *Western Christian Advocate*, was written by A. B. Leonard, D. D.:

"There appears to be no small amount of confusion in the minds of not a few, who ought to be perfectly clear, as to the action of the late General Conference on the question of caste in the Churches and schools of the Methodist Episcopal Church. The action of that body was of such a character as to put the whole question beyond the realm of doubt.

"On May 22, 1884, Report No. 3 was presented by the chairman of the Freedmen's Committee to the General Conference, and was adopted with but little discussion, almost without opposition. The third resolution of that report was as follows:

"'*Resolved, That the question of separate or mixed schools we consider one of expediency, which is to be left to the choice and administration of those on the ground and more immediately concerned: Provided*, there shall be no interference with the rights set forth in this preamble and these resolutions.'

"In regard to mixed schools and congregations the preamble said:

"'To the question of mixed schools we have given our most serious and prayerful attention. It is a subject beset with peculiar difficulties. That the colored man has a just and equal right, not only to life and liberty, but also to the means of grace and facilities for education, we not only admit, but most positively affirm. We are in duty bound to provide for and to secure to every class of our membership, so far as possible, a fair and equal opportunity in Church and school accommodations. And in so far as this is done our duty is performed, and the equal rights justly demanded of us thus fairly and fully conceded. *Mixed congregations and mixed schools may, in many places, be most desirable and best for all concerned. In other cases one class or the other, or both, may prefer separate congregations and separate schools.* Equal rights to the best facilities for intellectual and spiritual culture; equal rights in the eligibility to every posittion of honor and trust, and equal rights in the exercise of a free and unconstrained choice in all social relations, is a principle at once American, Methodistic, and Scriptural.'

" Upon a more thorough examination of the italicised parts of this report it was feared by many that it would justify *forcible* separation on the color-line where ' those on the ground' saw fit to adopt that policy. In the light of recent events that fear was well founded. The Chattanooga University trustees have done just what it was feared might be done under the resolution and preamble above quoted. If no further action had been taken by the General Conference, that body would be compelled to bear the responsibility of the rejection of colored students by the Chattanooga authorities. In the absence of further action the trustees could say that the ' question of separate or mixed schools' is 'one of expediency, which is to be left to the choice and administration of those on the ground.' 'We are *on the ground,* and we hold that *expediency* requires that colored students shall be excluded from our university, and we so decree.'

"But there was another General Conference committee that could properly consider and report on the question of caste—the Committee on the State of the Church—which had, according to the statement of its chairman, Governor Pattison, made upon the floor of the General Conference, given special attention to this question, even before the report from the Freedmen's

Committee was adopted. The unsatisfactory nature of the report from the Freedmen's Committee, already adopted, was regarded as sufficient reason why the report from the Committee on the State of the Church should be pressed upon the attention of the conference. That report was presented and adopted May 28th, the last day of the session. The report was as follows:

"'*Resolved*, That this General Conference declares the policy of the Methodist Episcopal Church to be, that no member of any society within the Church shall be excluded from 'public worship in any and every edifice of the denomination, and no student shall be excluded from instruction in any and every school under the supervision of the Church, because of race, color, or previous condition of servitude.'

"It was well known at the time that this latest action of the General Conference was intended to make it impossible under any circumstances, forcibly or morally, to 'exclude colored people from any Church or school under the control of the Methodist Episcopal Church.'

"The resolution was earnestly opposed by a small minority, and all parliamentary tactics were employed to prevent its adoption.

"Dr. Lanahan opposed it because the conference had already declared that 'color is no bar to any right or privilege of office or membership in the Methodist Episcopal Church,' and moved to postpone indefinitely.

"Rev. C. J. Howes moved to substitute a minority report, as follows:

"'*Resolved*, That there is no call for any farther action upon the relation of the races in our Church.'

"Brother Howes made a vigorous speech against the report and in favor of the substitute, at the close of which the previous question was ordered. Before the vote was taken, Governor Pattison, as chairman of the committee, made an earnest plea for the rejection of the substitute and the adoption of the resolution. The substitute was lost. A. Shinkle, a layman, called for a vote by orders, but the call was not sustained. The Rev. Dr..T. C. Carter called for a vote by orders, but the call was not sustained. The vote was then taken on indefinite postponement, and lost. A. Shinkle called for the yeas and nays, and the call was not sustained. The report of the committee was then adopted without amendment, a small minority voting against it.

"The adoption of this report, as narrated above, leaves no room for a doubt as to the position of the General Conference on the question of caste. There is no conflict between the two reports. The report from the Freedmen's Committee is to be interpreted in the light of the report from the Committee on the State of the Church.

"The attempt made by certain persons to make the impression that the latest deliverance of the General Conference was hasty and not well considered, is hardly less than a perversion of the facts in the case. Being the latest, it is the *mature* judgment of that body, and was intended to set at rest the question of caste.

"It is passing strange that any attempt should be made, particularly by members of the late General Conference, to justify the course pursued by the Chattanooga trustees. They have simply violated both the letter and the spirit of the deliverance of the Church through its only legislative body. There was but one thing, therefore, that the Freedmen's Aid Society could do without joining hands with the Chattanooga trustees; namely, to condemn their policy of rejecting colored students; and that, thank God, it has done. Let its resolution be engraved in letters of gold, and conspicuously displayed over the doors of all the schools under its care. Let it be announced boldly by bishops, editors, college faculties, and ministers, that the Methodist Episcopal Church knows no caste, either in its houses of worship or schools of learning.

"Now that this vexed question is settled, so far as it is possible to settle it by the action of the Freedmen's Aid Society, and settled in harmony with the action of the General Conference and the teachings of the New Testament, let the support of the society be more generous than ever before. There is no cause that is more worthy, and when its merits are fairly stated it can not fail to meet a generous response."

The following appeared in the *Western Christian Advocate* of same date, written by Isaac Crook, D. D. :

> "'You can and you can't,
> You shall and you sha'n't.'

"Allow a word now from one outside of the responsibilities of General Conference membership in 1884, and of ambitions for 1888, and with no votes to be defended. The action had on the report (No. 3) from the Freedmen's Aid Committee seemed to outsiders to say, 'That action is inspired by the prudence come from experience, and through those "on the ground."' It is in harmony with the liberty needful in all similar work North and South, and is sustained by the Pauline wisdom which 'took and circumcised Timothy because of the Jews in those quarters.' Local prejudices did control the 'policy' of St. Paul.

"The report of the Committee on the State of the Church (No. 4 adopted afterward) looked like a halt, and even a retreat, under some alarm at what had thus been done six days before.

"The first action said: 'The question of separate or mixed schools we consider one of expediency, which is to be left to the choice and administration of those on the ground.' That said, 'You can.'

"Then came, six days later, the adoption of this: 'No student *shall be excluded* in any and every school under supervision of the Church.' How could it say more clearly, 'You can't' 'exclude?' It is not now, as it was six days ago, 'left to the *choice* of those on the ground,' except as they choose to *admit.*

"When Lorenzo Dow would answer high Calvinism, which declared for the freedom of the human will, but that freedom possible only in one direction, he flung out the rhyme heading this article:

> 'You can and you can't,
> You shall and you sha'n't,
> You will and you won't;
> You'll be damned if you do,
> And be damned if you don't.'

"Is not Chattanooga University caught between the two horns of a parallel case of decreed liberty? 'Left to the choice and administration of those on the ground,' says Freedmen's Report, No. 3. Those on the ground administer for a white school under that General Conference '*can*,' when lo! they are caught by the younger member of the decrees governing the case, which says '*you can't.*'

"There is not a school under our Church-care in all the South but is liable to both horns of this dilemma of double decrees. No school in the North is so hampered.

"Let the next General Conference take out the Calvinism of the last action had, and adhere to that broad doctrine of human rights which allows not even the tyranny of any majority or minority, though it be of one headstrong person. Let us have freedom of election in both doctrine and polity, not to mention of delegates. May, the name of the beautiful month when General Conference meets, would make a good substitute for 'shall' and 'sha'n't' in all far-reaching legislation for distant and future contingencies.

"Those who show no faith in posterity, or people differently surrounded from themselves, provide for embarrassment and often for revolution. The antecedents and the present love of justice in the heart of Methodism may be trusted to see that every member of every color shall have right to the pursuit of 'life, liberty, and happiness,' with no other exclusions than a righteous Christian prudence may, as exceptions dictate, require. Even then the 'strong should bear the infirmities of the weak.'"

In the same paper, March 23, 1887, the following, contributed by Gershom Lease, appeared:

"That there should be a difference of opinion among good men, in so important a matter as our work in the South, is by no means strange. That even a General

Conference of grave divines and honored laymen, while navigating so dark a sea without compass or precedent, should occasionally run against breakers, is not to be wondered at. The only wonder is that, in twenty years of unremitting effort, the Church has not seriously embarrassed herself by her own action. The Church has had the wisdom and the grace to enter this unexplored field with her evangelizing agencies, and by her wisdom and success commend herself to the continued confidence of the people. For the first time in the history of this great work we are brought face to face with a problem, the solution of which is taxing the best thought of the Church, and exciting somewhat grave apprehensions in the minds of good men. The difficulty is in the interpretation of the action of the last General Conference upon our educational work in the South. It is not strange that there should be a difference of opinion; for there does really seem to be a want of harmony in the action of that body.

"On the nineteenth day of the session of the conference it adopted a carefully prepared report, presented by the Committee on Freedmen's Aid and Work in the Church on our educational work in the South. The third resolution of this report (No. 3) says that 'the question of separate or mixed schools we consider one of expediency, which is to be left to the choice and administration of those on the ground and more immediately concerned.' On the twenty-fourth day of the session the conference adopted a report presented by the Committee on the State of the Church, which declares the policy of the Church to be, that 'no student shall be excluded from instruction in any and every school under the supervision of the Church, because of race, color, or previous condition of servitude.' These two resolutions do not seem to be in harmony; each declares a distinct and different policy. The one declares the policy of the Church to be, that 'no student shall be excluded from instruction in any of our institutions of learning,' while the other just as distinctly declares that the 'question of mixed schools is one of expediency, to be determined by those on the ground.' How it is possible to harmonize these two resolutions it is certainly difficult to see. The theory that the one provides for the admission of a sprinkling of colored students into a white school is not satisfactory. This interpretation still leaves the question open, what per cent of sprinkling can be accommodated; which, in effect, breaks down the theory. Neither is it satisfactory to say that mixed schools is the policy of the Church, and separate schools the exception. Though this exposition might be preferable to the former, still it does not materially affect the situation; for the exception is left to the judgment of the parties 'on the ground and more immediately interested,' which is equivalent to saying that any of our schools may be exclusive, which is just what Report No. 3 declares.

"The two resolutions, then, declaring a separate and distinct policy, it becomes a simple question of *weight* between them. It can not be fairly said that the practical policy of the Church has been mixed schools or Churches; so that the resolution of the Committee on the State of the Church embodies a principle that has only had a shadow of application in the practical work of the Church; and the reason for it is founded in the fact that, after a fair trial, mixed schools and Churches have been found inexpedient. The preamble of Report No. 3 of the Committee on Freedmen's Aid declares that the 'establishment of schools for our white membership' 'has greatly redounded to the benefit of our colored people.' The resolution, then, so far as it declares for a uniform policy is not in harmony with that principle of practical expediency that we have found necessary in our work in the South.

"Again, the report of the Committee on the State of the Church seems to have been volunteered. It was not necessarily binding on that committee to prepare and present a report on that subject.

"And, further, the necessity for such a report seems to have been questionable. The position and policy of the Church, as to the equal rights of the colored man, had been sufficiently declared by the general policy and administration of the Church for the last twenty years. The policy of the Church in its Discipline and administration has been, and still is, to grant to the colored man all the rights, privileges, honors, and immunities of the white man. On the question of personal rights the Church knows no difference. He is the peer in Methodism of the white man in Church membership, in all the councils of the Church, and as eligible to any position of honor or trust in the gift of the Church as the white man. No resolution of the General Conference of 1884 could in any way dignify either the man or his equality of rights in the Church above that which he already enjoyed in the fundamental organism of the Church. There seems to have been no necessity for this action. It can be of no practical utility to the colored man.

"After the passage of Report No. 3 of the Committee on Freedmen's Aid, it could do nothing but invite conflict and embarrass the Church in its work. With all due respect to any action of the General Conference, the report of the Committee on Freedmen's Aid seems to carry with it a greater weight of obligation than the other. This committee was specially charged by the General Conference with the investigation of this subject. In fact, this was the object of the committee. The report itself shows that the committee appreciated the gravity of the situation, and thoroughly considered the extent and magnitude of the work, as well as the embarrassments because of race and color that have met the Church in the past. It embodies the godly judgment of the most thorough and painstaking investigation of any body of men authorized to speak upon that subject. This report is the deliberate and specially-provided-for judgment of the Methodist Episcopal Church upon this subject, and consequently carries with it all the weight that the deliberate action of the highest council of the Church can give it. Add to this the fact that it is in harmony with the practical policy of the Church founded in experience, and it seems to carry a weight with it, a force of authority, that would at least relieve a faculty and board of trustees that acted under it, of that severe censure that the authorities at Chattanooga have been subjected to. This would seem to be specially the case where an institution had been erected with the distinct understanding that it was for a particular race. We can but regard the action at Chattanooga as within the provision of authority. To waive all question of superiority, the action of the

General Conference under which they acted is of equal authority with the other. The other view of the case practically annuls Report No. 3, and leaves it a dead letter.

"While we would certainly entertain all due respect for the deliberate judgment of the 'board of managers of the Freedmen's Aid Society,' as set forth in their late action, yet we would respectfully submit that the *intentions* of the board as therein set forth, to dissolve its connection with the university, provided the local authorities do not rescind their action, may be hasty and unwarranted. The action proposed is one of serious import, which, if carried into effect, ought to have a clear and unchallenged justification."

The *Central Christian Advocate* of March 9, 1887, said:

"A few weeks ago we expressed the opinion that the Chattanooga University case would not be settled until the next General Conference. We thought there was ground, untenable indeed, for the position of the trustees, and that they would have a hearing before that body, and then the question of 'separate' schools would be discussed on its merits, and the Southern side would have the opportunity of presenting its views. But the action of the trustees and faculty in regard to Professor Caulkins revealed a state of affairs that no one suspected, and for which there was no defense from any point of view whatever. So great a misapprehension of the feeling and conviction of the Church in regard to her colored members had never occurred before. The path of duty was so plain that no one should have had a moment's doubt about it, nor should the university for one moment have hesitated to follow the suggestion of the authorities of the Freedmen's Aid Society. But the university party could not so see it, and declined to dismiss the offensive professor. This placed the whole affair in a new light, and the board of managers of the society were literally compelled to take the action set forth in their report which we printed last week.

"That they will have the support of the Church there can be no doubt. For while the Church may be willing to yield something to prejudice and custom, and agree that some of its schools may be properly classified as white, and others as colored, it will not sacrifice the principle of equality of rights among its members. No General Conference could be convened that would rescind the action of the last General Conference, when it declared that no student shall be excluded from 'instruction in any and every school under the supervision of the Church because of race, color, or previous condition of servitude.' We do not call in question the desire of the authorities of the Chattanooga University to secure the highest interest of the Church and of the two races. They do not design to perpetuate caste, but to bridge over the present till a better condition shall be established; and the Church intended to assist them in so worthy a work. But they did not take into account, as they should have done, the feeling of the Church. They misinterpreted the phrase 'expediency,' when they attempted to establish a rule which excluded all colored persons from the university.

"We regret that they did not put to the actual test their conviction, that the admission of colored students of the class that could claim entrance to a school of its grade 'would be fatal to the prosperity of the institution.' There are many persons who do not believe this. They do not doubt the honesty of the university authorities, but believe that they have taken counsel of their fears. They believe it possible to maintain a university in the South under the same conditions as in the North. This would have gone far towards settling the question, for some years at least. As it is, the question has to be taken up again under less favorable conditions for its determination. But we shall not fail in the end. So long as our hearts are right, blunder as we may, we will make certain progress in the right direction; for this question of justice and equal rights to the colored race has been thrust upon us by God himself, and he will lead us on, if we will suffer ourselves to be led, to a decision that will be approved in heaven."

The *Northwestern Advocate* of March 2, 1887, contained the following by J. B. Stair :

" Dr. Smart, in a short article on the caste question, asks some very pertinent questions concerning our Church in the South, but does not answer them so satisfactorily. The implication, however, is that we are there because the Methodist Church already there is so permeated by that 'devilish' and 'unfraternal spirit' [of caste] 'worthy to be accursed of God and good men,' that she can no longer do efficient evangelistic work. It would seem that a Church so afflicted would not only be incapacitated for any good, but would necessarily be without the pale of fellowship with any other Christian body; and yet somehow we continue to recognize our Southern sister as one of us, send to and receive from her Christian and fraternal greetings on every proper occasion, receive her pastors into our pulpits, hang by the thousands upon their words, profit numerically and spiritually by their labors, and devote half pages of our great Church weeklies to an advertisement of their sermons. Are we justified in thus figuratively taking to our arms a Church possessed of a spirit ' worthy to be accursed of God '—a Church whose course is so radically incompetent and wrong that able missions from our own Church are demanded to counteract it? If somebody can, will he please point out the consistency in all this? If we are in the South to convert people to our view of the caste question, we are there for a laudable purpose perhaps, but one doomed to failure. That question was not involved in Adam's fall, nor is our view of it necessary to salvation. If the politicians among us would stop a moment and consider the fact that caste exists elsewhere than in the South, and with reference to the colored race, it might at least furnish us with the occasion to divide our missionary forces with a view to a better distribution. Perhaps no country under Christian influence is more painfully afflicted with this ' curse' than England is, and yet Dr. Smart evidently fails to find a reason for sending missionaries there. True, the Negro is not there involved, nor are ante and post bellum rivalries; but that ought not to be an essential circumstance. The fact seems to be that caste exists about everywhere, even in our own dear Church. We have, and might again see, a form of it manifested, should the powers that be so far forget themselves as to send a doctor of divinity to a three hundred-dollar appointment in the backwoods; and instances are not beyond our own ken in which good Methodist families persistently forget to ask the servants to eat with them in the dining-room, even when the table is not crowded. It is remarkable how much color and climate have to do with the question of caste. Social relations, morally clean, are not a fit subject for the missionary works of a great Church. The legitimacy of our errand in the South will depend much upon the question whether we find there territory unoccupied, or whether we are there as rivals merely, of a Church with whom we have long been at political swords' points. Politicians, Church or other, should not be allowed to decide. If we are in the South, as are other evangelical Churches, for the purpose of saving the souls of men, we deserve Godspeed. But if the only reason we can give for being there is to eradicate caste, social prejudice between races, the foundation for our errand will deservedly be alike unsubstantial with its completed results."

The intention in thus presenting the Chattanooga affair, like that of the rest of this work, has been to sustain the facts: (1) There has never been a disposition on the part of the Methodist Episcopal Church to ignore its obligations to the colored man, but it has, in every conceivable way, aided him intellectually, financially, and spiritually. (2.) That the Church, as such, has always not only respected his manhood, but encouraged him, where circumstances or previous condition persuaded him to believe he possessed none, to respect his manhood and feel himself somebody. (3) That the Methodist Episcopal Church, as such, has done this to a greater degree, and with as much, if not more, consistency than *any other Church in this country, and at greater cost.* It is quite a different thing to say that she has always declared that *none but mixed schools* should be supported by the Freedmen's Aid Society. The simple and unambiguous statement, "the question of separate or mixed schools is one of expediency, which is to be left to those on the ground and more immediately concerned," forever excludes any such idea. If the mind of the Church can be known at all, it certainly is best known by the enactments of the several General Conferences on this question. From these we conclude that it is not the policy of the Church to truckle to caste prejudice in any form anywhere. It has declared that as a Church it favors "equal rights to the best facilities for intellectual and spiritual culture, equal rights in the eligibility to every position of honor and trust, and equal rights in the exercise of a free and unconstrained choice in all social relations." But the whole is greater than any part; therefore there is not, nor can there be, any Church or school conducted under the auspices of the Methodist Episcopal Church into which *any member or pupil* may not enter, or from which any proper person can be excluded "on account of race, color, or previous condition of servitude." This is the declared policy of the Church; also, the letter of the law on this question. The apostle Paul, a man of profound learning and great piety, as well as keen foresight—a man that so spurned caste prejudice as to withstand his brother Peter to his face concerning caste—says: "All things are lawful unto me, but all things are not expedient. The letter killeth, but the spirit quickeneth." It is true of the colored man in the Methodist Episcopal Church that "*all things are lawful*" unto him that are lawful unto any other man within the Church. It is equally true for the colored man that "all things are not expedient" for him any more than they are for white men within the Church.

We do not believe, nor do we wish to believe, that our Church intended, by anything done in the General Conference of 1884, or desired at that time to annul any of its hitherto impartial acts; to give any particular class of its members any indulgence in wrong-doing; to yield to any kind of race or class prejudice; that it attempted or desired to elevate any class of its members above another; or, on the other hand, that, while it slept, an enemy sowed "tares" in the field. We think no one believes that it was the intention of the Church to dishearten or disband or leave to themselves the schools among our white membership in the South, organized and conducted, as well as supported in part, by conferences of our Church, in the which *there are no colored members.* The Church must have seen and felt that *it is an utter impossibility* for

any Church, indeed for the United States government, to mix promiscuously, perforce, the schools
in the South; that if the two races there are to be
educated by our Church, in some sort they must
be allowed a "free and unconstrained choice in all
social matters." Rome was not built in a day. Dis-
eases that have become chronic, and remain within a
system for two hundred and fifty-eight years, can not
be eradicated in a month, even though an entire
college of physicians attempt it. When the Church
requested the Freedmen's Aid Society "to give such
aid to the above-named schools during the next
quadrennium as can be done without embarrassment to the schools among the freedmen," it recognized not only the *existence* of exclusively white
schools, but provided *for their perpetuation.* The
situation of affairs is peculiar indeed. The above
action was not intended (though we candidly believe that those who claimed the opposite had a
right to, and did think so) to recognize the right
to exclude *any pupil* on account of race, color, or
previous condition, on the plea of exercising their
"free and unconstrained choice." That General
Conference, however, *did intend to allow the two races
in the South to have the privilege of separate schools,*
if they desired them, as it had not interposed objection to separate annual conferences. As proof of
this, the General Conference put the entire educational work of the Church in the South under the
direct management of the Freedmen's Aid Society.

The wisdom of this, to our mind, does not appear on the surface; for, if the Church should at any time in the future call a colored man to the office of corresponding or assistant corresponding secretary in that society, Banquo's ghost will rise again. Again, it was made, and is now, the duty of each pastor, when asking for collections or presenting the claims of the society, to state plainly that "the funds collected are to be used for both races, and where contributors express the desire, they shall be allowed to say where their funds shall go." Here, again, we come face to face with a knotty problem as to the wisest method evenly to balance those funds. It is natural to suppose that *the prejudiced class* in each race will turn all funds into the channel into which his prejudices run. Now, to keep even financially, the two races within the Church in the South must do one of two things, viz.: Either drop the question of races, and let the funds collected be proportionately appropriated, or keep up the race question, and thus keep their funds separate. Which will be done? Does it require the wisdom of a philosopher to guess? Neither can, under the present *régime*, without financial loss, afford to be *less prejudiced* than the other; for the reason that the funds raised by the unprejudiced class will be equally divided, and it will get only its part of *its collection*, while the prejudiced class will not only receive its *own collections* but an *equal proportion of the unprejudiced class's funds.*

These complications are but the legitimate out-growth of the animated discussions in the General Conference of 1884 touching the race question. We do not believe the Church intends to lessen its interest, lag in its zeal, or retard the progress and prosperity, or circumscribe the usefulness of our schools where only colored pupils have chosen to matriculate, or to allow the children of our white membership in the South to grow up in ignorance and superstition while it is able materially to succor both at the same time and in the same way. Is this view not reasonable, equitable, and best? Is it not a reflection upon Methodism to view it otherwise, in the light of the past history of the Church on the race question? While we say "in the same way," we do not intend to say in the same school-building or recitation-room. To-day it certainly appears utterly impossible to mix promiscuously our Church schools in the South after having founded one class of them upon *an entirely different basis.* It might be done in the North. Might it not? We can not, however, argue along the same lines for Church schools of any denomination for any particular class of students in the South that we can for those in the North. The two cases are as dissimilar ecclesiastically as the two sections of country are politically.

The training has been different. In the first place, the relations of the two races in the two sections have always been, and are to-day, different;

the training of the whites in both these sections has been different—a different class of text-books, as well as a different class of teachers, who were educated differently; the changed relations of the two races in late years from master and servant to citizen and freeman, and the *modus operandi* of the other Churches which are engaged in the same work in the South. What Church, engaged in the education of the colored man in the South, does not maintain separate schools for the colored and white? Not because they favor caste, nor because they think it would not be better, if possible, to educate them together, but they are doing the best they can under the circumstances. There may be beautiful exceptions, but they are exceptions few and far between. I am sorry it is true; but *'t is true.* The promiscuous mixing of our Church schools in the South, if practicable, would now be inconsistent in the face of our separate conferences. There are two influences in the South to-day that are coeval with it—and we came near saying co-eternal—that are as despicable as invincible; the one is the misasma of the swamps, and the other is caste prejudice. Neither the wisdom nor skill of physicians has been able to overcome the one, nor the armies of Cæsar nor of Christ have been able to eradicate the other. Death—the common leveler—has thus far been the only *sure* remedy. But why frown at this when you remember that the latter of these evils finds congenial soil, if not some cultivation, in some Northern latitudes? If up North it is "the arrow that flieth by night," we should no tbe surprised to find it "the pestilence that walketh at noonday" in the South. While all this, and more, is true concerning caste, it does not, for a moment, lessen the crime in the South because it crops out now and then in the North.

When we contemplate caste in all its blackest and most disgusting phases, we grow sick at heart, and feel as if we would like to snatch it out, top, root, and all; but then we remember it may be that in doing so we might draw up a beard of wheat. We believe, however, that as our membership in the South, of both races, get more and more under the light of the cross, and farther away from "slavery days," they come. nearer together; the more harmony that exists between the two in their efforts to educate themselves and elevate those about them, and with whom they have influence, the more potent factors in the evangelization of the world they become. No sane colored man within the Methodist Episcopal Church believes that it would benefit his race if the Church were to give up all its work in the South among the whites. Nor is it just fair to believe that the colored man is in and remains with the Methodist Episcopal Church for her "loaves and fishes." It also appears that we as colored men in the Church must be on the alert lest we be pushed up to the point of antagonizing all our Church work in the South, save that among

ART DEPARTMENT OF CLAFLIN UNIVERSITY.

and for ourselves. Following the action of the board
of managers of the Freedmen's Aid Society the Lexington Annual Conference unanimously indorsed the
following action, and requested its publication in
the Church papers, showing one phase of this
question, viz.:

"The results attained by the Freedmen's Aid Society since its organization are marvelous, viewed from
every point. The work of this society in the country,
Christianizing, elevating, and educating the people, can
not be expressed in figures or told in words. Wherever
its schools have been established the condition of the
people has been bettered and public sentiment liberal-
ized. Too much in the way of praise and thankfulness
can not be said of this benevolent organization of our
Church and its officers, and we earnestly commend its
objects and work to the thoughtful consideration of our
ministers and people, satisfied that the more thoroughly
the operations of the society are understood, the more
hearty the support it will receive.

"As to the Chattanooga troubles, and other matters
of the same nature, we beg to say:

"We do not believe it is right to yield the time-
honored opinions and views of the Church as to the
equality, brotherhood, and perfect freedom of man, nor
that a line of action should be pursued by the society or
Church to secure the favor or countenance of those
whose life-teachings are inimical to the position of our
Church, and who really have no objection whatever to
the Negro, so that his relation to them is a servile one.

"We desire and pray for the success of all our

schools in the South that are under the fostering care of the Freedmen's Aid Society, but not at the loss of the manhood and self-respect of our race. Having been long satisfied that this question would come up for solution and settlement, and now that it is before the Church, we are heartily in favor of the Church going steadily and faithfully forward in the path pointed out for it by the Master, regardless of prejudice, local or otherwise. Compromise will only delay the day of settlement, and gain not a single point for God or humanity.

"Objections are made to the mixing. of white and Negro pupils in the same Church schools, and it is said that there are as good schools for Negroes as the society provides for whites. Various other reasons are given favoring this view of the question. For us to admit that these objections to the children of Negroes attending the Church schools with whites are of sufficient force to lead us to be governed by them, is to admit our own inferiority, and the necessity of such a separation from our white brethren as to end in the putting out of the Church of every Negro member in it. If we admit discrimination as being proper here, we ask, where will it end? Whatever may be the opinion of others upon the subject, as to its expediency, etc., we can have but one opinion, and that is, that we are members cf the Methodist Episcopal Church, yield to none in devotion and loyalty to that Church, and can not admit that it is injudicious or impolitic to send our sons and daughters to any of the schools of the Church.

"Christianity is colorless, and Christianity demands of the Church that it shall not recognize the exclusion of any of its members from any of its communities or schools by reason of rank in society or of race characteristics, especially when this exclusion carries with it a mark of degradation. The General Conference has given this principle expression.

"We do not believe it well for this conference to remain silent upon this subject, when its silence may be construed into an indorsement of the unholy sentiment that it is proper to bow before this baseless prejudice, which is a relic of slavery. We believe this question will be settled, as all other questions have been settled which tended to elevate the Negro, and we believe the Church will firmly adhere to Christian principles, and lay aside everything that has the appearance of mere policy."

CHAPTER XIV.

WHAT WILL THE HARVEST BE?

AFTER the examination we have made, and trying to scan the future, we see what has been gained by the colored members who remained in the Methodist Episcopal Church. They have been admitted to full membership, to communion at her altars, official relation as laymen, given work in the pastorate, presiding elderate, and given to understand that "color is no bar to an election to the episcopacy."

> "But these attained, we tremble to survey
> The growing labors of the lengthened way;
> The increasing prospect tires our wandering eyes;
> Hills peep o'er hills, and Alps on Alps arise."

Will a time ever come in the history of the Methodist Episcopal Church when she will tire of the race question, and abandon forever her work among and for the colored man? It is hardly conceivable that this will ever occur. The discussion of the race question becomes beautifully less at each General Conference. It is true that new phases develop now and then, and there follows a clash at arms; but it never, nowadays, amounts to more than a passage at arms, for the reason that the average agitator receives but comparatively little encouragement from those Churches in this country which have turned their backs upon the colored man. They tremblingly hope the Methodist Episcopal Church *will* make some awkward step that will eventually drive the colored man out; but they have seen her stand by him in the hottest contests unflinchingly, and in the face of a gainsaying prejudice that is as old as the venerated Constitution and as deep rooted as sin, and they fear to say yea or nay touching what it will or will not do. The Methodist Episcopal Church can never forsake the colored man, and be consistent. It declared in 1816, 1844, 1861, and 1872, by its actions, that the duty of the Christian Church was to stand by the colored man, by making him feel at home within it as much as possible. Now to go back, would be to say that the Church South in 1844 was right in defending slavery, and right in ridding itself of the colored man in 1870, and that that which the Methodist Episcopal Church did at those periods was wrong. This it can never do, and be consistent.

One other question at this juncture arises. It is one fraught with much interest, as it is one that would involve the entire eight millions of colored people in this country, that would naturally widen the chasm between the white and colored races in this country, and would sustain the same relation to a war of races in this country that the separation of the Methodist Episcopal Church, South, sustained in 1844 to the war of the Rebellion. It is, Will the colored members within the Methodist Episcopal Church eventually be separated from it? If the existing relations between the Church and her colored members remain as they are now, No. There could be no reason for a separation, since "there is no word white" known within the letter of the law of the Church to indorse invidious distinctions "on account of race, color, or previous condition of servitude;" there are no privileges accorded to any man of one race in the Church, that another of any other race within the Church is not entitled to *by law*. There is no church-building with the name of the Methodist Episcopal Church inscribed upon it, into which any person "having a desire to flee the wrath to come" may not go as a worshiper, or become a member. This is also true of any university, college, or school under the auspices of the Church. There is no annual conference of the Church to which the colored man has not a perfect right to belong; no position within the gift of the Methodist Episcopal Church, from janitor to bishop, to which any member, white or colored, may not aspire, be elected or appointed to, and discharge the functions pertaining thereto, without hindrance. In a word, the white and colored membership within the Church is, according to the enactments of the General Conference, equal in all that pertains to Church membership and privileges. Hence there is now no cause for the colored membership seeking separation from the Church. "We know not what a day may bring forth;" but, judging the future by the past, there will never come a time when it will be *absolutely necessary* for the Church to put away its colored membership, nor *an absolute necessity* for the colored membership to withdraw from the Church. The question of the inferiority of the colored man within the Church to the average white member within the Church, is fast disappearing, whether we speak of this in reference to General or annual conferences. The Methodist Episcopal Church is turning out enough young colored men from her universities, colleges, and schools, from Boston to Austin, Texas, each year, *to form an annual conference.* The graduates from her schools are everywhere joining the Church and conferences, and, to a certain extent, coping with those whose chances have been more favorable. No absolute necessity for separation exists, and, for that matter, may never exist. May it not be found more profitable, after a short time, for all the colored Methodists in this country to unite and form *one grand united body of colored Methodists?* This question has been urged by many different parties, with as many different motives at the bottom. Let us notice a few. In "Our Brother in Black" (by Dr. A. G. Haygood, of the Methodist Episcopal Church, South,) at page 226, we find the following touching the point at issue:

"The most remarkable tendency that has so far shown itself in the development of their ecclesiastical life is the strong and, as I think, resistless disposition in those of like faith to come together in their religious organizations. The centripetal is stronger than the centrifugal force. We have already a number of African Churches. Indeed, the great majority of them belong to Churches not only of their own 'faith and order,' but of their own 'race and color.' . . . This disposition has become very pronounced, and has expressed itself on a very large scale since they were set free."

At page 236 the good Doctor reaches his point when he says:

"If every colored Methodist in the United States were to-day in one organization, this would not change the grounds or nature of our obligations to them in any respect, so far as fraternal love, fraternal aid, and co-operation are concerned. It would then, as now, be our duty to help them in all possible ways; and considering their history in this country, and the providential indications of their relation to the salvation of Africa, just as much our duty then as now. If there were not one Negro in the Methodist Episcopal Church the Freedmen's Aid Society would be as much needed as it is now. 'The colored Methodist Episcopal Church of America' that was 'set up'— I hope not 'set off'—needs the help of its mother, the Methodist Episcopal Church, South, every whit as much as if they were still with us. Nay, all the more, because they are not with us. And we ought, before God, to help them." We simply add, *it is about time.*

In a book written by a layman of our Church, John A. Wright, of Philadelphia, with the title, "People and Preachers in the Methodist Episcopal Church," at pages 262–6, touching the question of separation, he says:

"A conclusive argument in favor of separation would be made if it could be satisfactorily proven that the connection as it now exists is injurious and demoralizing to both parties; if it could be shown that their presence is a danger, and has a corrupting influence on the main body of the Church; and that such separation could be made without injury to the colored man. There has been an unwillingness, a hesitation on the part of the Church to discuss this question, but the undoubted use that was made of the colored votes in the last General Conference (1884) to secure places was so patent to every careful observer that it can not be kept down. The ease with which the influence and votes of these innocent and generally very ignorant representatives were secured by those nearest to them, shows how great a danger there would be in the abuse of the confidence placed by them in their avowed friends.

"There are important movements among the colored people that should be noted. All will remember the enthusiastic patriotism, civil and religious, which was to abolish all color-lines and all laws that recognized black and white, or their intermediate shades. Yet a law of nature, of race, and of common sense is asserting itself among the colored people, in that they want to be separated from such close connection with the white man. They feel that there is an incongruity, an unfitness, a something that causes them to desire to be free from his presence and government. They have but little respect for the whites who remain among them. It is a growing belief among the more intelligent colored people that their religious growth would be increased by their independence of the white Church. So strong is this feeling in certain places, that a secession from the Methodist Episcopal Church, and the formation of independent Methodist Churches, is seriously discussed. In obedience to this growing sentiment, the General Conference, in 1884, recognized the policy of basing membership of annual conferences on a color-line. An argument in favor of caution in treating this question may be drawn from the relation of the colored people to the interests of the country. The colored vote in the United States is accepted as a source of danger in the future to this country. The present colored vote, as it has or has not had the privilege of free expression, has determined who should be President of the United States. . . . It may or may not be an idle fear, but wise men are looking at the question in sober earnestness. . . . The Church, then, should be carefully guarded against danger arising from the presence of so large a colored mem-

bership through the use of its power in the General
Conference. The idea of separation for better work
is not new among us. We have the German and
colored conferences, and would have Scandinavian
if there were enough Scandinavians. There is a
law of association that is the best regulator of such
questions. That a separation into conferences on
the color-line will become general is inevitable.
The questions will come up before the General
Conference to decide, whether the colored ministers
can be so educated as to continue in the Methodist Episcopal Church without any serious danger
to its interests; if not, the lesser must suffer, if suffering it would be, for the sake of the greater; or
whether, when they are prepared, they will not do
more good by being transferred to some branch of
the African Methodist Episcopal Church.

"There are the African, the Zion, and the Colored Methodist Episcopal Churches, which last was
wisely set apart by the Southern Methodist Episcopal Church at the end of the war. They are all
strong, aggressive, and independent Churches. If
the members of these Churches could be united
with the colored members of the Methodist Episcopal Church they would make a membership of
nearly one million of people. What an opportunity for usefulness to their race would be thus
placed before them! It must be admitted that their
continued connection with the Methodist Episcopal
Church does not tend to promote their dependence

upon themselves. Government aid makes a restless pauper class; Church support has the same tendency. That the two races do not work well together, or rather that the colored Churches do not prosper when intimately connected with white Churches, is pretty well exemplified in the city of Philadelphia, where the only two colored Churches, living side by side with the large white Church membership of that city, had so dwindled in numbers and financial ability in 1884 that the Church Extension Society had, practically, to purchase two churches for their use, so that the colored brethren from the South might have a Church home when they came to the General Conference. During the same time the African and the Zion Methodist Episcopal Churches have been very successful in that city, have done much good, have able bishops, leaders, and a respectable membership. On the one side there was dependency, and on the other independency. It is risking but little to assert that the number, character, and self-reliance of the members of the colored Methodist Episcopal Church, South, are far greater and better than they would have been if their connection had continued with the old Church.

"A further thought deserves consideration at this point. If the colored members are to be continued in the Church, or as long as such connection may last, would it not be to the interests of all parties to dissolve the annual conferences in which they are in a large majority, and form them into mission conferences, as they were prior to the General Conference of 1868, without a voting representation in the General Conference? By doing this the Church would be saved from the low average grade of intelligence of the General Conference of 1884, caused by the presence of nearly forty of such representatives, and from the corrupting influences that were so palpable. The colored people would then understand that their connection was not permanent, but was in the line of educating them to take care of themselves. 'In the meantime the Church could continue its good work in giving them the advantages of education, training in trades, and to the most promising a fitting education for the ministry and learned professions. The suggestions made hereinbefore as to the proper basis of representation in the General Conference, connected with that of the last paragraph, would reduce the number of delegates to the General Conference from the colored conferences, and thereby lessen the danger. It is important that this or some other protective plan should be adopted before the separation that is inevitable between the white and colored work takes place. No mere pride of numbers or prestige should have any influence to prevent the Church from saying to the colored brethren, 'Go in peace, and may the God of heaven protect and guide you;' and with this benediction handing over to them all the churches, colleges, and property that have been accumulated for their use."

The sequel will show that the writer of that book knows but little concerning the colored people. Let us for a moment stop and look more closely at the above chapter from Brother Wright's facile pen. There is no mistake, Brother Wright has in some way had his plans *upset.* That he intended to "get even" with some one is also apparent. This general attacks first one and then the other division of the grand army of Methodism. First he attacks the army at large for neglecting to bring more laymen to the van. He then charges upon the clerical regiment, declaring it is in the way of his "consummation devoutly to be wished." Being somewhat repulsed, he falls back in disorder, only to find the colored regiment supporting, in some sort, the former. At once his guns are leveled, and he makes a Fort Pillow charge upon "the black brigade." Of this brigade, within the Methodist army, he declares: " A conclusive argument for separation would be made if it were proven that the connection existing [between the white and colored people] within the Church is injurious to both classes." He attempts to prove the proposition, by declaring that, by the presence of colored representatives from Southern and mixed conferences, "but few are fitted for their places and are still grossly immoral," in the General Conference "grades down the intelligence and wisdom of the whole body, to a level too low for safety; that the ease with which the influence and votes of these innocent, and generally very ignorant, representatives were secured by those nearest to them, shows how great a danger there would be in the abuse of the confidence placed by them in their avowed friends." The gentleman should not have stayed so far away from those "innocent and generally very ignorant representatives." Knowing, as he must, that the man whose intelligence gives him advantage, even in a Methodist General Conference, over "the innocent and generally very ignorant" is the greater sinner, he strikes at "the avowed friends" of the colored man. But in a great many instances some of the "avowed friends" of the colored man in the General Conference of 1884 were those whom Methodism, within and without this country, "*delights* to honor." But aside from this, it were well for the good brother had the revisers of the Old Testament elided the "thou shalt not bear false witness."

We question very much whether a single *proper* delegate to that General Conference was "innocent and generally very ignorant" enough to miss the truth as far as he seems to have missed it, and for the same purpose. He also says: "The colored men feel that there is an incongruity, an unfitness, a something that causes them to desire to be freed from his presence and government. They have but little respect for the whites who remain among them." If that is so, it is *too bad.* If it is not so, then—? When a witness testifies to one thing, and then contradicts himself, if he is adjudged sane, the court will throw out his testimony, declaring him either ignorant of the truth of the facts he would relate, or else a perjurer. If the former, he should be reprimanded for meddling with matters he knew nothing about; if the latter, the law would punish him. If the colored men within the Methodist Episcopal Church feel "that there is an incongruity, a something that causes them to desire to be freed from his presence [the white man] and government," it could arise from no better source than that such men persist in remaining within the Church who abuse them.

"They have but little respect for the whites that remain among them." We think no man who understands our work in the South will deny that Drs. J. C. Hartzell, J. Braden, and A. Webster, "remain among them." But Dr. Hartzell was for five years or more the secretary of the Louisiana Conference, where the colored men are in the majority. He has repeatedly been elected to the General Conference by his brethren, and usually on the *first ballot.* Rev. John Braden, D. D., president of the Central Tennessee College, at Nashville, Tennessee, has been there for nearly twenty years, and as a member of the Tennessee Conference has been treated by his conference brethren like Dr. Hartzell, of Louisiana Conference. Dr. Alonzo Webster, of the South Carolina Conference, being, we believe, *the only white man* in it, has been treated by his conference brethren just as the brethren of the Tennessee Conference treated Dr. Braden. Without multiplying illustrations, we ask, what becomes of Brother Wright's argument? It follows, that his darts fall futile at the door of a Church that by law knows "no word white."

Again: "The General Conference must yet decide whether colored ministers can be educated so as to continue in the Church. If not, the lesser [the colored man, of course] must suffer; or whether, when they are prepared, they will not do more good by being transferred to some branch of the African Church" When did our bishops receive authority to "transfer" ministers into another Church? When the time for that transferring comes, would not the members of the General and annual conferences be privileged to vote upon it?

In speaking of the three colored organizations, the African, African Zion, and Colored Methodist Episcopal Churches, he says: "They are all strong, aggressive, and independent. The last was wisely set apart by the Methodist Episcopal Church, South, at the end of the war." The *African Methodist Recorder*, of July, 1887, contained an article signed by Rev. J. H. Welch, of that Church on "Union of Colored Methodists in this Country." The facts there stated have not been called into question, not even by the editor. So that the facts stated stand unquestioned. In speaking of the African Methodist Episcopal, the African Zion Methodist Episcopal, and the Colored Methodist Episcopal Churches of America, the very ones spoken of by Brother Wright, he says:

"But as we stand to-day separated, all of us are weak and inefficient. In almost every city, town, and village, each branch of the Methodist family has planted a Church, and in many places neither of the Churches can give the pastor a comfortable support. Neither of the branches above referred to has a first-class institution of learning nor an efficient corps of professors and teachers; and those we have are just existing, and that is all. Neither of these organizations has a missionary system operating as it should. Neither branch of these Methodist bodies has a first-class book concern."

Now, the above comes from an African Methodist of the African Methodists—a man conversant with the inner and outer workings of the machinery of the three "strong, progressive, and independent" colored Churches. Who is right, Brother Wright? As to the wisdom displayed by the Methodist Episcopal Church, South, in setting apart its colored daughter, we leave Dr. A. G. Haygood to say, as he has at page 236 in "Our Brother in Black." However, the aforesaid brother missed it a few years, when he says "set apart at the end of the war," for it was not "set apart" until 1870. But then, you know, a few years—say seven—don't

amount to much when we have an object in view.
At last he feels as if a solution of his troublesome
problem has been reached. When speaking further
of the three "strong, aggressive, and independent
Churches," he says: "If the members of these
Churches could be united with the colored members
of the Methodist Episcopal Church, they would
make a million of people. What an opportunity
for usefulness to their race would be thus placed
before them!" It's wonderful, is it not? At this
point the good brother reaches his *climax*. By all
means, let it be done! Let us begin now! Come,
let us go up to the next General Conference of our
Church, and pass a law that all the colored Methodists in America and Canada *must come into our
Church*—bishops, elders, exhorters, and laymen—
and thus accept the magnanimous "opportunity for
usefulness to our race." What would the good
brother *then* think of General Conference representation? Would he have it reduced? But fearing
that some others may not see the plan as he sees it,
he says: "If they [the colored members] are to
remain in the Church, would it not be to the
interest of all parties to dissolve the annual conferences in which colored members are in the
majority, into mission conferences? If not, then
reduce the number of colored delegates." Now,
any one can judge from what we have cited from
the book, just about how much credence should be
had *in anything* the book, "Preachers and People

in the Methodist Episcopal Church," has presented. And yet it does show that the question of a separation from the Methodist Episcopal Church is being discussed; for even the. author of that book has a backing within and without the Methodist Episcopal Church, for he is one of the leading officials in the Arch Street Methodist Episcopal Church, Philadelphia.

Caste prejudice has not been, but will yet be, driven to the owls and bats, before the onrolling tidal wave of intelligence and sober common sense that is even now breaking upon the shores of this country. And yet it does seem as if there is but one of two ways in which it can be done, or by a combination (suiting the case) of the two,—the hump of caste prejudice now resting so adroitly upon the back of our American Protestant ecclesiasticism must be amputated by the impartial but keen blade of the great Physician; or Protestantism must bow so low in the dust and ashes of humiliation, that this unsightly protuberance shall be visible no more forever. Then, and not till then, can we hope to see this camel go unscathed through the eye of the gospel needle.

CHAPTER XV.

UNION OF COLORED METHODISTS.

WHAT would be the result of such a union? If an organic union of all the colored Methodists in America could be effected, it would make no mean Church. Just think of the African Methodist Episcopal, the African Methodist Episcopal Zion, the Colored Methodist Episcopal Church in America, and the colored members now within the Methodist Episcopal Church, say to the number of three hundred thousand, uniting and forming one Church, composed of 22,076 ministers and a membership of 1,012,300, bringing with them an army of Sunday-school children not far from 1,500,000 ! If the divine promise were fulfilled in each of these, that "one shall chase a thousand and two shall put ten thousand to flight," why, such an army of true believers could, as the quaint preacher said, "shake hell to its center" while moving the world toward the cross of Christ!

It was in 1883 when Dr. Tanner, through the columns of the paper he was then editing, the *Christian Recorder*, of the African Methodist Episcopal Church, suggested the idea of an organic union of all the exclusively colored organizations. A year or so ago the colored Methodists of Canada, under Bishop Nazery, united with the African Methodist Episcopal Church. It did not amount to much then nor since. Several times overtures have been made to the two other colored Churches by the African Methodist Episcopal Church, but it has usually ended in talk. The fact may as well be stated first as last, that a time will never come in the history of this country when all the colored Methodists will belong to *one great Negro Church.* In the first place, the African Methodist Episcopal, the African Methodist Episcopal Zion, the Colored Methodist Episcopal Church of America, and the colored members of the Methodist Episcopal Church, each and every one of these is looking forward to, and praying for, a time when *all* the others will come back to mother or come over and live with sister. Again, because the separate and distinct colored Church organizations have been warring with each other from the beginning of their organization, and these old feuds and petty jealousies keep coming up every time organic union is mentioned. It can not occur, because the African Methodist Episcopal and African Methodist Episcopal Zion Churches continued separate before the war, and when it ended expected to, and did, receive a wonderful influx from the Methodist Episcopal and Methodist Episcopal Church, South. Those two organizations saw a few apples still clinging to the parent tree in the South. They began throwing sticks and mud, then they tried "taffy," and then stones.

In 1869 each of the above-named two Churches began to get ready for the reception of the one hundred thousand members then in the Church South. As the General Conference of the Church South in 1870 met, each of those denominations, basing its faith on the repeated promises of many of the prominent preachers of the Church South, began to prepare to receive them. They were chagrined, however, when, instead of "coming over," they marched out into the broad field of independency, and set up shop for themselves by the assistance of the Church South. The two older Churches then began to bushwhack all they possibly could, seizing "every straggling soul as their own *lawful* prey." The two larger colored organizations will not unite, because each is still waiting and expecting her younger sister to visit and remain with her. The three will not unite, because each is expecting a time to come when the three hundred thousand colored members of the Methodist Episcopal Church will leave in a body and join it.

Of course, the colored members of the Methodist Episcopal Church are praised, abused, loved, laughed at, or coquetted, as the case seems to require at the time. It is really amusing at times to hear the stories told—good, bad, and indifferent—by these three organizations, to induce our members to come. And yet, somehow or other, the one does not seem to know why the other should anticipate our coming. We can not see it. Before we had separate confereuces it did look as if all our members would be stolen from us. But every day now the colored members of the Methodist Episcopal Church pitch their tent a day's march farther from any kind of African Methodism, on the one hand, and from having the oceans circumscribe them by joining "The Colored Methodist Episcopal Church of, or in, America." If there ever comes a time in the history of the colored members of the Methodist Episcopal Church when it will be no longer useful, pleasant, or wise to remain, they will undoubtedly *form another colored organization, and man it themselves.* They have the material. There is no colored Church in this country that is educating so many young people a year as the Methodist Episcopal Church. Our brethren of the three colored organizations in this country will tell you that the time has now passed when their bishops, General Conference officers, etc., can visit the Commencement exercises of our schools and colleges, and take away in their pockets, by flattery or promises, our young people as they were wont to do. This is the explanation of the mushroom "universities and colleges" under the auspices of certain "powers" in this country. Our young men and women begin now to see, as do many others, that a time not far distant *must come* when the best outlook for cultured colored men and women will not be, as some would have us believe, in Africa, nor among the Africans. Why should it not be a separate

GAMMON THEOLOGICAL SEMINARY, ATLANTA, GA.
(LIBRARY BUILDING.)

organization of our own, if any change *must* come? Indeed, the thought presents *the most flattering prospect,*—the twenty or thirty universities, colleges, normal schools, and academies given into the hands of our own competent presidents, professors, and teachers; the real estate, consisting of college buildings, churches, and parsonages, with mortgage on only about twenty-five cents on the dollar; five hundred thousand children in our schools, and over three hundred thousand members, with the great Methodist Episcopal Church behind them! Now and then some good brother, like the author of "Preachers and People in the Methodist Episcopal Church," advances the utopian idea of handing us over to some one of the existing colored organizations, but the good men and women in the Methodist Episcopal Church are hoping for no such thing. We believe the good men and women predominate.

In the above-referred-to book the statement is made that "the more intelligent colored people in the Methodist Episcopal Church are seriously thinking of separating from the Methodist Episcopal Church." If the poll were taken of every intelligent colored man within the Church, such an idea would be laughed at, for no such feeling prevails. There is no such spirit abroad within the Church on the part of *the colored members.* If it exists at all, *it must be sought elsewhere.* There is no occasion for it; and though it may be that now and then some word is let fall by some braggadocio, that if so and so is not done, thus and so will happen, yet no such stuff has ever fallen from the lips of the leaders of our colored membership, properly so called. Should anything of the kind ever be broached, there would be no occasion for secrecy, and less for braggadocio; no absolute necessity for rejoicing on the part of *any* colored organizations, if there might follow overtures to the Methodist Episcopal Church for organic union that are not now made. The thought naturally uppermost at this juncture in the minds of some may be, Would it not be Christian-like and brotherly for the colored members to separate, so that organic union may take place between the "two great branches of Methodism in this country?" *Is that what keeps them apart?* We would, to the question as to separation, answer, No. If we understand the heart of the Church—and we think we do, having been born naturally and supernaturally in her lap—she does not ask as much. In 1844 the Church, by dropping her interests in and work for the colored man, could very easily and knowingly have preserved her union, power, and influence, kept back the rebellion for a time, received the encomiums instead of the vituperation and obloquy of every slaveholding nation in the world, and brought to her support the strong slave oligarchy of the South. She did not do it. She will never compromise with sin enough to accept even an organic union conceived in caste and born of a hate that excludes *one* the Lord said should be loved as herself.   We believe, laying aside all personal predilections, prejudice, and aspirations that, so far as the Church is concerned, the colored members of the Methodist Episcopal Church will remain therein until they are pleased to go out, if that is until the sound of the first trumpet.

Would there be anything gained by a separation? To our mind there is nothing to gain, and much to lose, by the colored members of the Methodist Episcopal Church separating from it.   In the first place, it would have the same tendency that the now existing colored organizations have, casting reflections upon the wisdom of those good men and women who all along have contended for general equality; it would weaken the race politically and socially; widen, instead of narrowing, the chasm between the white and colored clergy in this country. "Like priests, like people," would naturally widen the breach between the laity.   This would naturally cause variance between neighbors because of color. This would naturally lead to separate schools where they are now mixed, and keep forever separate those that are now separate.   In a word, it would magnify caste, race prejudice, and eventually lead to a war of races.   The segregation of one million or more colored men in this country into *one single organization* would endanger the safety of our Republic in more ways than one.   In the second place, a separation now from the Methodist Episcopal

Church for *anything less than a crime against the race* would not only be suicidal, but foolhardy, paying kindness with contumely, and subjecting not only the members concerned, but the race to the scorn and laughter of the world. We do not expect to have everything go our way, to count for more than we number, nor to see every law we propose adopted, nor to be fondly dandled in the lap of an affectionate and opulent mother. We expect only what we have always received from the Church—the privilege of *full membership therein.*

The work which the Church has done in the South, may be seen from the following tables:

BOARD OF EDUCATION UP TO JANUARY 1, 1887.

NAME.	Pupils aided.	AMOUNT.	LOCATION.
Centenary Bib'l Institute.	46	$1,850 00	Baltimore, Md.
Central Tenn. College .	67	2,446 00	Nashville, Tenn.
Claflin University . . .	45	2,015 00	Orangeburg, S. C.
Clark University	12	732 00	Atlanta, Ga.
Cookman Institute . . .	4	158 00	Jacksonville, Fla.
Bennett Seminary . . .	6	200 00	Greensboro, N. C.
Gammon Theol. School .	29	1,663 00	Atlanta, Ga.
Haven Normal Institute.	3	75 00	Waynesboro, Ga.
Morristown Seminary .	22	755 00	Morristown, Tenn.
New Orleans University.	44	2,327 00	New Orleans, La.
Philander Smith	5	228 00	Little Rock, Ark.
Rust University	11	400 00	Holly Spr'gs, Miss.
Rust Normal Institute .	2	75 00	Huntsville, Ala.
Wiley University . . .	18	855 00	Marshall, Texas.
West Texas Conf. Sem. .	5	140 00	Houston, Texas.
Total	319	$13,919 00	
In Northern Colleges . .	6	2,000 00	
Grand Total	325	$15,919 00	

WORK OF CHURCH EXTENSION SOCIETY.

Expended to colored membership by donation . $237,000 00
Expended to colored membership by loan 150,000 00

Total given by Church $387,000 00
Total given by colored members by collection . . 35,000 00

Amount received by colored members more
    than they raised $352,000 00
Churches this saved, built, or helped to build for them, 2,000.

WORK OF THE MISSIONARY SOCIETY SINCE THE WAR.

Conference.	Amount.	Conference.	Amount.
Central Alabama .	$16,600 00	Savannah	$20,250 00
Delaware	23,438 89	South Carolina . .	49,217 25
Florida	20,228 65	Tennessee	34,236 78
Georgia	38,571 58	Texas	32,103 09
Lexington	27,053 50	Washington	55,833 68
Louisiana	126,201 50	Little Rock	12,700 00
Mississippi	155,943 63	Colored work in	
Missouri	42,486 06	Kansas	7,500 00
North Carolina . .	25,622 45		
St. Louis	41,279 00	Total	$729,266 06

In the above figures the West Texas Conference is included in Texas Conference, East Tennessee in the Tennessee Conference, etc. While no claim is set up that the above figures are exactly true, they are at least an approximation. Where the conference was mixed, one-eighth of the missionary appropriation only has been credited to the colored work, though it is easy to see how mistakes could creep in an account of this. But the work that has been done, and the interest which the Church has had in it are apparent. So long as souls are to be saved, the Church can not relax its efforts toward these people, whether white or colored.

THE WORK OF THE SUNDAY-SCHOOL UNION.

The great work done by this benevolent society
of the Church among the colored people of the
South deserves emphatic mention in connection
with these tables of results which we have been
giving. It will be impossible to tabulate perfectly
statistical results among the colored people, as the
work done has been for the populations of the
South, regardless of color, and has so interpen-
etrated that it would be impossible to say that this
was done for one race, and this for another. We
may mention, however, the publication of the
Good Tidings and its gratuitous distribution among
the Sunday-schools of the colored people in the
South. During the year 1888 the Sunday-school
Union, in connection with the Tract Society, sent the
Good Tidings to 2,536 Sunday-schools in 807 different charges in the Southern States. The weekly average of *Good Tidings* distributed was 37,134 ; total
number of copies distributed during the year,
1,994,000; total number of pages, 7,976,000. No
one can possibly estimate the great good which has
been accomplished by the circulation of this excellent publication. Besides this, the Union has sent
grants of Sunday-school libraries, music-books,
catechisms, and Sunday-school periodicals of every
possible description to all parts of the South, calling into existence new schools, and inspiring discouraged schools with new life. Possibly the most

helpful work accomplished by this society has been its personal visitation in the person of its efficient agents in all parts of the South. Almost every section of the country has been touched. Extensive campaigns of work have been conducted. Weary and disheartened pastors have been encouraged; new schools have been organized, which have already grown into commanding churches; new and better methods of work have been taught a people who knew so little how to work; and because of this "hand-to-hand" effort immense good has been accomplished, and the Sunday-school Union stands well to the front among the benevolent societies of the Church, contributing to the growth of the Methodist Episcopal Church among the colored people of the South.

In addition to this official work for the Sunday-schools of the South, there were in several places organized efforts to collect and distribute second-hand books in needy localities. From Cincinnati many boxes of these were forwarded, that useful reading matter and school-books might be supplied by the proper agents to those who had not the means to purchase for themselves. These went largely into the cabins and cottages of the freedmen; and the first lessons in reading were learned by many who had no other teachers than those in the Sunday-schools. A single book served ofttimes for an entire family. Father, mother, and children were alike ignorant, and alike needed instruction.

THE FREEDMEN'S AID AND SOUTHERN EDUCATION SOCIETY.

Institutions among Colored People.

1. Collegiate. Teachers Students

	Teachers	Students
Centenary Biblical Institute, Baltimore, Md.	12	223
Central Tennessee College, Nashville, Tenn.	22	545
Claflin University, Orangeburg, S. C.	23	946
Clark University, Atlanta, Ga.	23	340
New Orleans University, New Orleans, La.	15	266
Philander Smith College, Little Rock, Ark.	12	185
Rust University, Holly Springs, Miss.	10	355
Wiley University, Marshall, Texas	17	230

2. Theological.

Gammon Theological Seminary, Atlanta, Ga.	4	71

3. Biblical Departments.

Baker Institute, Claflin University	6	10
Centenary Biblical Institute (correspondence 6)	3	31
Central Tennessee College (correspondence 62)	2	102
Gilbert Haven School of Theology, New Orleans	3	15

4. Medical and Dental.

Meharry Medical College, Nashville, Tenn.	11	55
Medical Department New Orleans University (just organized)	5	
Meharry Dental College, Nashville, Tenn.	8	11

5. Legal.

School, Central Tennessee College	6	6

6. Industrial.

Claflin College of Agriculture and Mechanics Inst., Orangeburg, S. C.	20	507
John F. Slater Schools of Industry, Nashville, Tenn.	8	194
Schools of Industry, New Orleans University	2	120
Schools of Industry, Rust University, Holly Springs, Miss.	4	35
Schools of Industry, Centenary Biblical Institute, Baltimore, Md.	4	53
Manual Training-school, Philander Smith College, Little Rock, Ark.	4	92
Industrial School, Bennett Seminary	3	11

	Teachers.	Students.
Schools of Industry, Wiley University, Marshall, Texas	4	116
Schools of Industry, in Cookman Institute, Jacksonville, Fla.	2	18
Schools of Industry, Gilbert Seminary, Baldwin, La.	7	75
Classes in Huntsville Normal Institute, Huntsville, Ala.	2	27
Schools in Clark University, Atlanta, Ga.	10	204

7. Academic.

	Teachers.	Students.
Bennett Seminary, Greensboro, N. C.	6	125
Baltimore City Academy, Baltimore, Md.*		
Central Alabama Academy, Huntsville, Ala.	4	140
Cookman Institute, Jacksonville, Fla.	6	321
Delaware Conference Academy, Princess Anne, Md.*		
Gilbert Seminary, Winsted, La.	17	299
Haven Normal School, Waynesboro, Ga.	3	153
LaGrange Seminary, LaGrange, Ga.	3	209
Meridian Academy, Meridian, Miss.	3	154
Morristown Seminary, Morristown, Tenn.	9	260
Samuel Houston College, Austin, Texas (not opened last year)		
West Tennessee Seminary, Mason, Tenn.	2	149

** Teachers and Students counted in Centenary Biblical Institute.*

INSTITUTIONS AMONG WHITE PEOPLE.

1. Collegiate.

	Teachers.	Students.
Chattanooga University, Chattanooga, Tenn.	9	161
Grant Memorial University, Athens, Tenn.	18	291
Little Rock University, Little Rock, Ark.	14	266
Texas Wesleyan College	10	240

2. Theological.

	Teachers.	Students.
School, Chattanooga University	2	13
School, Grant Memorial University	3	27

3. Legal.

	Teachers.	Students.
Class, Grant Memorial University	1	41
Class, Little Rock University	6	20

4. Academic.

	Teachers.	Students.
Baldwin Seminary, Baldwin, La.	2	56
Bloomington College, Bloomington, Tenn.	4	138

	Teachers.	Students.
Ellijay Seminary, Ellijay, Ga.	3	151
Graham Academy, Smyrna, N. C.	3	86
Holston Academy, New Market, Tenn.	2	90
Kingsley Seminary, Bloomingdale, Tenn.	4	131
Leicest r Seminary, Leicester, N. C.	4	136
Mallalieu Academy, Kinsey, Ala.	2	65
McLemoresville Institute, McLemoresville, Tenn.	7	114
Mt. Zion Seminary, Mt. Zion, Ga.	4	140
Powell's Valley, Well Spring, Tenn.	4	175
Parrottsville Academy, Parrottsville, Tenn.	3	125
Roanoke Academy, Roanoke, Va. (not opened past year)		
Trapp Hill Academy, Trapp Hill, N. C.	2	125
Warren College, Chucky City, Tenn.	4	155
Woodland Academy, Cumberland, Miss.	2	72

RECAPITULATION.

GRADE OF SCHOOLS.	Among Colored People.			Among White People.			Total.		
	Number...	Teachers...	Students...	Number...	Teachers...	Students...	Number...	Teachers...	Students...
Collegiate	8	134	3,090	4	51	958	12	146	4,048
Theological Seminary	1	4	71	......	......	......	1	4	71
Biblical Departments	4	14	158	2	5	40	6	19	198
Medical Departments	2	11	55	......	......	......	2	11	55
Dental Department	1	8	11	......	......	......	1	8	11
Legal Department	1	6	6	2	7	61	3	13	67
Industrial Departments	12	70	1,455	......	......	......	12	70	1,455
Academies	12	60	1,810	16	54	1,759	28	114	3,569
Totals.*	21	223	4,971	20	105	2,717	41	328	7,688

* In these totals students and teachers are counted but once; and departments are *not* counted as separate institutions.

In twenty-two years the Freedmen's Aid and Southern Education Society has expended in the work of Christian education in the South about $2,500,000.

The present value of the property owned by the Society in the South is over $1,500,000. This includes lands—some of which have increased in value—school buildings, furniture, and libraries. More than one hundred thousand colored students have been in the various schools, and a reasonable estimate is, that the preachers and teachers in public and private schools, from among this multitude, have had under their influence fully one million of the youth and adults of the South. No words can adequately express the far-reaching and glorious results already achieved, and yet to flow, from this ever-widening current of intellectual and moral power.

THE DUTY OF THE HOUR.

With the understanding that we are not cumbersome to the Church, what is the duty of the colored members therein? It is our indispensable duty to remain loyal, wise, and prudent. By saying that the colored members of the Methodist Episcopal Church ought to remain loyal, does not necessarily carry with it a thought that there is a spirit of disloyalty brewing. What is intended is simply that each and every member thereof should know his and her obligations to the Church, her rules and regulations, and sacredly keep them, "not for wrath, but for conscience' sake." If the entire membership would be loyal and stay loyal, as well as appear loyal in the eyes of the world and of the Church, it must see to it that there is no just ground for such complaints against the race as have hereinbefore been mentioned as found in Mr. Wright's book. The charges he brought forward were, that the colored delegates to the General Conference of 1884 were "generally very ignorant representatives." He said also: "It is said, by those who know and judge impartially, that to-day there are but few men in any of the Southern colored and mixed conferences who are fitted for their places, and that the colored members are still grossly immoral." These are *awfully* serious charges, whether true or not. A great many people in these United States will probably form (or may have already) an opinion from that book of not only the race with which they anon come in contact in the busy scenes of every-day life, but of the colored membership of the Methodist Episcopal Church, members of the same Christian family, who are privileged to eat at the same Lord's table. We know there are thousands of chances for *even us* to say, "It is not all on this side of the house;" but it makes but little, if anything, in our favor if others are no better than we. That the good brother overleaped the bounds of reason, not to say common sense, in his desperation to make out a case, is a foregone conclusion. What he says is, that "those who know and judge impartially," say "that the colored members are still grossly immoral." What a fearful charge is this against the bishops of our Church, that they have brought into the Church, directly or indirectly, under their very noses, *three hundred thousand* "grossly immoral" members! Thousands of these have received authority to preach the gospel and administer the sacrament of the Lord's Supper; none of whom have been less than two years under the almost personal training of the General Conference. Is n't it horrible? Who believes it? But no one need be surprised at this tirade against the poor " black man," for in his next paragraph above, at page 265, brother Wright, in speaking of the white ministers and agents sent South to teach the colored people, says: " The general impudence and lack of knowledge of the agents and ministers sent to the South have blocked up the way of the Church. The *immoral character* and the dishonest practices of some inflicted disgrace on the Church and cast a doubt on all." All the white delegates were not as " learned " as the author of " Preachers and People in the Methodist Episcopal Church," who were elected to attend the General Conference in 1884. It was not to have been expected that *all* the colored delegates would measure up to him. However far he may have missed the truth in this case, intentionally or otherwise, one of the best ways for the colored members in the Church to show that they are loyal and worthy is to elect *no one* as a delegate to the General Conference who is not qualified. By qualified we mean possessing natural and acquired ability, and the grace of God richly shed abroad in the heart. With the former he will be qualified to discharge the functions of his office with credit to himself, his race, and the Church. By the latter he will be "an epistle known and read of all men," who will by it perceive that he is "neither common nor unclean," but "a workman that needeth not to be ashamed." As presiding elders, pastors, officers, and members of the Methodist Episcopal Church, let us let our light shine by raising our standard higher. Let no one be recommended for license to preach by us in any quarterly meeting, however far back in the woods it may be, who has not "gifts and grace." As to our mode of worship, let it be after the manner of our excellent Discipline, and not after the style of Revolutionary days. Let our Sabbath-schools be brought up to a higher plane. Let the songs of thanksgiving and praise, accompanied by the Word of God and prayer, be of daily occurrence where it has been periodical. Let us see to it that, as a Church, the rules and regulations thereof are kept to the very letter. Let us, as a race, continue to improve morally, financially, intellectually, and spiritually, "having an eye single to the glory of God." "Finally, my brethren, be strong in the Lord and in the power of his might. Put on the whole armor of God, that ye may be able to stand against the wiles of the devil. Stand therefore, having your loins girt about with truth, and having on the breast-plate of righteousness, and your feet shod with the preparation of the gospel of peace ; above all, taking the shield of faith, wherewith ye shall be able to quench all the fiery darts of the wicked.

And take the helmet of salvation, and the sword of the Spirit, which is the Word of God; praying always, with all prayers and supplications in the Spirit, and watching thereunto with all perseverance," until the great and notable day of the Lord, when you shall appear before the great white throne, and hear the Captain of your salvation, to the question, "Who are these?" answer, "These are they which came up out of great tribulation, and have washed their robes and made them white in the blood of the Lamb."